Endorsements

"I am thrilled with the down-to-earth manner in which Anthony describes his deliverance from drugs and alcohol. His story genuinely reflects the simplicity of the gospel of Jesus Christ, who came to earth to save, heal, and deliver us! I pray that those who read this book desiring freedom...may you find it in Jesus Christ!"

—Dr. Sheryl L. Price
Founding Co-Pastor
His Hands Ministries
Fellowship, Inc.[1]

"I love Anthony Ordille, and I love his story. This book is not only a testimony to the grace of God; it is a clear-cut guide to all who want to break addictions in their own lives. It's not just that we know people who need deliverance; most of us need it ourselves. Anthony's "way out" can be yours too."

—Larry Titus
President, Kingdom Global Ministries
Author, The Teleios Man[2]

An Injection of
FAITH

An Injection of
FAITH

One Addict's Journey to Deliverance

Anthony Ordille

An Injection of Faith
Copyright © 2018 by Anthony Ordille. All rights reserved.

Unless otherwise noted, all scripture is from the New King James Version of the Bible © 1982 by Thomas Nelson Inc. Used by permission. All rights reserved.

Scripture quotations are taken from the Amplified Bible. Copyright © 1954, 1958, 1962, 1964, 1965, 1987 by The Lockman Foundation. All rights reserved. Used by permission. www.lockman.org.

Inserts about how it works are taken from NA Narcotics Anonymous Fifth Edition,

Copyright © 1982, 1983, 1984, 1986, 1987, 1988 by Narcotics Anonymous World Services Inc. All rights reserved. www.na.org.

Scriptures used under Affirmations by The Sure Foundation Institute are taken from:

Scripture quotations from The Authorized (King James) Version. Rights in the Authorized Version in the United Kingdom are vested in the Crown. Reproduced by permission of the Crown's patentee, Cambridge University Press

No part of this publication may be reproduced, stored in a retrieval system, or transmitted by any means, electronic, mechanical, photocopy, recording, or otherwise, without the author's prior permission except as provided by USA copyright law.

This book details the author's personal experiences and opinions about addiction and recovery. The author is not a healthcare provider. This information is given to understand that neither the author, publisher, nor any associate of AFL is engaged in rendering legal, medical, or professional advice. In addition, the author, publisher, nor any associate of AFL does not represent or warrant that the information accessible via this book is accurate, complete, or current. Except as specifically stated in this book, neither the author, publisher, nor any associate of AFL, contributors, or other representatives will be liable for damages arising out of or in connection with the use of this book. You understand that this book is not intended as a substitute for consultation with a licensed healthcare practitioner, such as your physician. Before you begin any addiction recovery program or change your lifestyle in any way, you should consult your physician or another licensed healthcare practitioner for any treatment necessary for detoxification, or ensure that you are in good health and that the examples contained in this book will not harm you.

www.anthonyordille.com

Cover revision image provided by ©2021 Designer Pie. Ltd
Interior design by Jomar Ouano
Revised Book Layout © 2017 BookDesignTemplates.com

First published in the United States of America by Tate Publishing, October 2013, under ISBN: 9781627466820

Anthony Ordille published this revised edition in January 2018
ISBN: 978-0-99962-772-3 (Paperback)
ISBN: 978-0-99962-775-4 (eBook)
ISBN: 978-0-99962-776-1 (Hardback)

1. Biography & Autobiography / General
2. Religion: Spirituality / General
3. Self-Help / Substance Abuse & Addictions / Drugs
13.07.08

Dedication

First, I want to thank God, who gave the inspirational vision for the book, along with chapters, my Lord and the savior of my life, Jesus Christ, who is the backbone of my life, and the Holy Spirit, who led me through the memories of my life and helped me with the words.

This work is dedicated to my stepdaughter Michelle, who battled addiction and died of an overdose on May 16, 2005.

I want to thank my ex-wife, Laura, and son, Jarred, for their support and encouraging me to finish writing the book.

I would also like to thank Dale Hinz for proofreading the first printing and my family for their support at the end of my addiction.

Lastly, a special thanks to Dr. Sheryl L. Price and Larry Titus for their endorsements and Sam Jackson from Prints Charming Photography, Fort Worth, Texas.

Contents

Introduction 1
Chapter 1 3
   A Normal Childhood, I Think 3
Chapter 2 17
   Dreams, Visions, and Goals 17
Chapter 3 33
   How It All Started 33
Chapter 4 45
   Going Against the Current! 45
Chapter 5 55
   Let Me Out of Here! 55
Chapter 6 61
   Detox Time! 61
Chapter 7 65
   Why Am I Here & Where Am I Going? 65
Chapter 8 71
   Let's Do The Twelve-Step! 71
Chapter 9 79
   Being Taken Out of the Miry Clay! 79
Chapter 10 87
   I Can See Clearly Now! 87
Chapter 11 103
   Come and Go with Me! 103
Chapter 12 111
   Affirmations 111
Available Drug and Alcohol Program Hotlines: 136

Suicide Information 137
Resources 139
Other Books by this Author 140
Connect with Anthony Ordille 141
Photos 143

Introduction

The main reason for writing this book is the hope that it will help those who are struggling with addictions and show them that there is a way out. Most addicts are directed to a twelve-step program (rehab or some type of institution), which is acceptable to start your road to recovery, but there is another way. I have been there for over thirty-two years clean from drugs, and twenty-two years from alcohol, after relapse at my nine-year mark.

I served in leadership roles within the AA (Alcoholics Anonymous)[3] and NA (Narcotics Anonymous)[4] programs, holding speaking and chairman positions. I saw people I had loved not be able to stay clean, only to end up right back where they started. In chapter 8, I will explain why these programs are not the final answer. I will walk you through my life and how I ended up in the swamp of life, then how God delivered me out of that pit of filth, washed me as white as snow, and set me free from all addictions. He wants to do the same for you!

If I were in front of you, I would first say: "God loves you no matter how dirty you are or what you have done to yourself or anyone else." He is 'no respecter of persons' (Acts 10:34). If you open your heart and mind as you read this book, He will meet you right where you are, grab your hand, and pull you out of the miry clay. "He brought me up also out of a horrible pit, out of the miry clay, and set my feet upon a rock, and established my goings" (Psalm 40:2).

As you will see, it is your willingness to know the difference between what is right and what is wrong; what you read in this book is a guideline to your deliverance, and you should get your own Bible and read it for yourself so you can see how the word of God will change your life. Start with the book of John.

I will use the first chapters to set the stage for my life and then lead you into the addiction that once ruled it. Afterward, I will show you the road to my recovery and end with the truth, complete with testimonies.

Chapter 1

A Normal Childhood, I Think

I started my life as an average child in a lower-class family, with a dad who was a truck driver and a mom who was a housewife and also cleaned houses for a few people she was friends with. I was the youngest of six children, four boys and two girls, and even though my parents never divorced, our family could be what is called dysfunctional.

Webster's Dictionary[5] says *Dysfunctional* means the following:

1. Not operating normally or properly
2. Deviating from the norms of social behavior in a way regarded as bad

A dysfunctional family would be anything outside of the everyday lives of that old TV show, Ozzie & Harriet; at least they wanted us to think they were normal. It could also be parents who are on the verge of divorce. It could be dysfunctional to have an absent father or mother, leaving the appearance of a single-parent home, even if there is no divorce. Maybe it would be a family constantly arguing or physically fighting with one another or abusing their children.

A family with multiple conflicts, domestic violence, employment issues, and alcohol or drug abuse affects the family unit's basic needs. Anything that would make a family unstable could be added to this meaning.

I think most of today's families could be considered dysfunctional. It is hard to narrow down the true meaning of "A Dysfunctional Family" when we cannot recognize normal behavior in our society. Even though our family is far from this meaning, it still played havoc in my mind.

Even though I had come from a two-parent home for most of my childhood, my dad was never home; he was always working. Some days, I would be in bed when, just before midnight, I would hear the truck pull up and hear the psst from the airbrakes. Then I would fall asleep, and in what seemed to be minutes, I would hear the idling of that Mack engine, and I would turn to look at the clock to see that it would be around 4:00 a.m., and he would be off to do it all over again. So my dad was an absent dad in those early years, which played a big part in how I grew up.

Sometimes I think my brothers and I would get into trouble with our mom, so she would say, "Wait until your father gets home!" We would do that so that we would get to see what he looked like.

When my dad would get home, my mom would tell him about any trouble she had with us, and because my two brothers, who are four and six years older, and I would share a bedroom, he would come up and the one who caused the most trouble that day would get hit.

Please understand me; my dad did not beat us. I think he only did it to keep my mom quiet, even though one time I do recall my brother having a BB rifle, and he did something wrong, and my dad took that rifle and laid it across his knees, which broke not just the gun but one of my brother's knees as well.

I remember my older brothers trying to take the place of my dad not being around, and I would resent them for it. I wanted them to be my brothers and show me how to do things, not tell me what to do. It took me a long time to overcome this emotion and forgive them for trying to help out. I did not understand at a young age, but I understood why they did it as I got older.

My parents were dysfunctional in a way that, from the time I was born, they never slept together; my dad started sleeping on the sofa in the back living room. I think my mom was done having kids and did not want to take a chance on getting pregnant again; plus, she was in her forties when she had me.

My mom and dad were good parents; they never had the money to help us all be the best we could have been, nor did they understand what was needed to help us grow. They were old school, with hardly any education (I think they only made it to around sixth grade). They sent us to a Catholic school, made us attend church, at least my mom, and tried to instill Christian values. One of my sisters even went away to become a nun, but never finished. My brothers and I were altar boys and even talked about becoming priests. We even have cousins who are priests and nuns.

We had a two-story house with four rooms downstairs, three bedrooms, one bath upstairs, a basement, and an attic that only a tiny part could be used. The original part was built in the early 1900s with one room downstairs and a bedroom upstairs, and no bath or kitchen—they were outside. I am glad I was not born then! As time passed, three further additions were made, with another stairway added during one.

It was not a big house to start with, but it ended up being around 2,700 square feet. It had two staircases, which was fun because a few times when my dad would come home, when we were still awake, that is, we would run from him and go up one staircase, around to go down the other, and around and around again. Sometimes we would do it three or four times before my dad would give up, and I used to get a real kick out of it. Today, I know it was because it made me feel like a family.

As the youngest kid in the family, you would think I would have much love flowing down to me. I think it started that way because of some of the stories I heard, but I do not believe it ran throughout my childhood. My siblings most likely loved me, but no one knew how to show it or say it because we did not have a house of love. We never hugged each other, which brings me to the time that one of my brothers met his wife. When she came around, she would hug us, and some of the family would say things like, "Why does she have to hug us all the time?"

I loved it; it felt good to have someone hug me. I cannot speak for anyone else in my family, but I never heard my dad say he loved me until he was eighty-five, and I was thirty-eight years old. About three months before he died, my daughter approached me one evening and said, "Grandpop wants to see you."

I went downstairs and asked him what he wanted. He turned to me, put his hands out, which had a jar, and said, "This is for you."

I took it from him and saw it was filled with coins, nothing of real value, just some fifty-cent pieces, old nickels, and silver dollars, but to him, it was like handing me a million dollars. I asked him, "Why are you giving these to me now?"

He said, "Because I love you, my boy."

I turned and went upstairs because we were getting ready to go to the movies and running late; then, as I was driving down the road, it hit me. I realized what had just taken place, and I started to cry. I cried so hard that I could not drive. My dad had just told me he loved me for the first time! It was so pleasing to my ears! I know God used those words to help me to forgive my dad for not telling me any sooner.

I wanted to tell my dad how much it hurt me, not hearing it sooner, but one of my sponsors from Narcotics Anonymous told me I could not tell a dying man that, so I did not.

Talking about tough love, having to grow up, and never hearing the words, I love you, is a tricky thing to overcome. Praise God; I do not hate my dad anymore; he died as my friend.

Not only did I grow up hating my dad for not telling me he loved me, but I also hated him for not being there for me to do things with me, like a lot of the other kids' dads were. I remember my brothers being on the Little League hardball team, and we would see them play. But when it came time for me to be of age to join, I had no way to get there because my dad was working, and my mom never got her license. They would not let me ride my bike to the lake, so I had to quit.

I did get to go with my dad on the road from time to time, and oh, how big it would make me feel! I felt like I was riding on top of the world in that Mack truck, high off the ground, looking down at everything. We would sit there without talking for a few hours, but I did not care because I was enjoying just being with him for a kid whose dad was not around much. I will talk about one of those trips in the next chapter because I was so proud of how my dad handled a dire situation that, to this day, amazes me.

As I got older, my dad's work was not as hectic, so he would be around a little more on weekends, allowing him to do more, which I could enjoy being with him. He went to his sister's and brother's houses for a while until his sister died. Then, for some reason, he stopped talking to his brother for a while, so that stopped. I never did find out why they stopped talking since my dad never explained things to me.

I would run out to him and ask if I could go with him, even though there was nothing for me to do there, except that my aunt would be cooking the Sunday meal. I loved her meatballs; they were the best in the world. I still have not had any, not even my mom's, that tasted like hers. She would let me eat all I wanted as she would tell my dad, "Charlie, aren't you feeding this boy? Look how skinny he is!" Then she would say, mangiare (eat) in Italian.

I used to be a beanpole, and no matter how much I ate, I never gained any weight. But as an old-school Italian lady, she thought everyone should be fat. Over at my uncle's, he would let me play the piano. Outside of that, there was nothing for me to do. He only had one child, and she was much older than I, so I would walk around the garden or the grape fields or maybe go inside and play the piano.

We were not dysfunctional from our mom or dad being drunks or anything like that, so I did not inherit my addiction. I never saw my mom drink anything with alcohol; I only saw my dad drink twice. Being from an Italian town, during the holidays, when the wine (known to us as Dago Red) was ready, he might go to our neighbors to tap the barrel a few times, but never enough to be tagged a drunk.

As a young kid, I would set up a model train set for Christmas. I would put a 4'×8' sheet of plywood on the floor to build my model city. One time, I was almost done with my setup; it was one of those few times my dad came home drunk. He went around the corner to go up the steps, lost his balance, and fell into my miniature city. The remarkable thing was that I usually put the train along the back wall, and he missed them. Which was a good thing because they were Lionel trains and were worth money.

It was not until my late teens/early twenties that he would be around more, and by that time, I had my own thing going on, and it was not the same. I will share how this affected me as a dad in later chapters. I wanted to point out that even though my dad did not say the words, *I love you*, he sometimes showed it in his actions. Like: when I had my construction business, sometimes he would come to the job site and hang out and maybe even bring me some lunch.

You would think that being in a large family, I would have been able to fill my time with my siblings, and I wanted to, but as a young boy, I would hear, "You are too young. Go home!"

I heard this as I followed them down the street. I wanted to hang with my brothers, yet that is what I would get time after time. So I had to find things to do alone, making me a loner.

I know that I did have time with my brothers walking to school, but it was not quality time, and today, we do not talk as often as I would like. I love them and know they love me, but we never grew to depend on one another because of the lack of bonding as kids. If I could do it all over again, that is one area in my life I would change. I think each of us knows that what I just wrote about is true, but we never did anything to change it, and as we got older, we might have thought it was too late to change it. One thing I am learning while walking in Christ is that it is never too late for anything as long as all involved are willing.

When I got mad at one of my brothers, I stole a twenty-dollar bill from him. I think I was in first or second grade, bringing it with me to school to buy candy. When I got to the cashier, she called a teacher, who asked me where I got the money. I could not tell her I had stolen it, so I had to lie and say my mother had given it to me. How did I know she would call home to ask my mom? Since we only lived about half a mile from school, my mom walked there to give me a good beating. I never stole anything from him again, but that day, I planted a seed of thievery and lying, which grew in my later years.

As I grew older, I started to see that my two brothers, the only ones left in the house, were drifting further away from me because everyone else was on their own. I was losing hope that I would be part of their lives. However, I would get to play baseball with them and their friends from time to time whenever they played on our field. Even with that, I would cling to my mom more because she was the only one who seemed to be around.

I would play games with myself, like army, cards, watch TV, play with my trains, and any other toys I got my hands on, or play catch by throwing the ball at the porch steps. I did have two girls who were neighbors, and they were around my age. So as I got older, my mom would let me go over and play with them. My mom had a friend who had a girl my age whom I used to play with as well. Even in high school, everyone thought of us as cousins because of our proximity. Also, I had a third cousin from out of town that I would spend time with whenever my parents visited. I think that because of all these girls in my past, today I feel more at home being with a group of women than I do with a group of men.

I would get laughed at and called names like mommy's boy and sissy, but I did not care because at least I had someone who would listen to me and wipe away my tears. I found a picture of my mom and dad sitting at a table at a party, and I was standing next to my mom instead of playing. I know this sounds like it may be abnormal, but to a little kid who feels rejected by his siblings, an absent dad, and no other boys in the neighborhood to play with, she was all I had.

My family was so poor that, as the youngest kid, I would have to wear my brother's clothes. Sometimes, they were too short, and everyone at school (and I do mean 98 percent of my class) would make fun of me and would say things like:

"Anthony, are you expecting a flood today?"

"Anthony's family is so poor that he has to wear his brother's clothes!"

"Anthony, if you keep growing, you can wear them for shorts!"

I would just run away and hide and hope to die. They would also make fun of my ears and how they reached a point and stuck out. By the time I was fourteen, I had started to grow my hair to cover them. When I was in third grade, I told my mom I wanted to transfer to public school because I failed, but the truth is, I used that as an excuse to change classmates, thinking that would change how I was treated. Oh, if you want to know why I failed, it was because I had received a 69 (F) instead of a 70 (D) in English/Spelling, and I blamed the teacher instead of myself. I find it hard to write even to this day.

It seemed that no matter what I did, nobody wanted to be my friend, and I grew up thinking it was because I was ugly or because of my name and who I was or was not. I did get to change schools, but not until seventh grade, and it did get a little better for me because I was working, and I could buy my clothes, and my brother stopped growing, so his clothes fit me better. By this time, I would wear his clothes not because I had to but because he allowed me to, at least most of the time.

I want to make a note here; if you are calling people names, stop it; it does nothing to them but harm and can take them years to overcome—that is, if they overcome it at all. You know that old saying, "Sticks and stones may break my bones, but words will never harm me." Well, it is one of the biggest lies ever and is from the pit of hell. The devil (yes, there is a devil) comes to steal, kill, and destroy (see John 10:10).

Bones will heal easier than the harm words will do, and if you have been hurt by words spoken to you, I have some good news. The second part of that verse says that "I, (God), came that they [meaning you], may have and enjoy life and have it in abundance." Awesome!

One day, when I was around twelve, I saw some people moving in across the street, and as I was watching, I saw boys running around. I was so excited; I ran to my mom, telling her what I saw. I asked her, "Do you think they are moving in?"

"I do not know, Anthony. You will have to go over to find out," she replied.

"Can I go now?" I said with excitement!

She said, "Yes, but be careful crossing the street."

So I went over and stood there until one of the boys introduced himself and said, "What is your name?" That was the start of what seemed to be the best time of my life until it turned on me. You see the first…oh, I would say, two years, everything was going great. I would go over to the house almost every night and all weekend, and when there was no school, I would be there all day. I would eat there, and they made me part of the family, especially when their mom remarried, and the man called me one of his kids.

It was just like Robert Kiyosaki, who wrote *Rich Dad Poor Dad*. I, too, had a friend with a rich dad; he was there for me when my dad was not and showed me how to do things. At that time, he was the only male figure, outside of my brother-in-law, who was in my life who was teaching me stuff. I loved that man like a dad, and I even called him my dad, number 2.

When he was dying from cancer, I would go over to the house to sit by his bed to pray with him and be there just in case he needed me, as I needed him. One of the best things he did for me was when he sat me down one night when I wanted to quit school. I was in the tenth grade then, and he told me how important it was for me to graduate and that if I did not want to do it for myself, I would do it for my mom. I respected his word, so I stayed in school and am so grateful I listened. He was heaven-sent, and I thank God he was part of my life.

Back to having those boys as friends, there were four of them. We would have fun going to the movies, driving my dad's car in the field around our house (and sometimes around the block), playing baseball, riding our bikes all over town and to the lake, and going to the beach (which is about the only time I got to go as a kid because once I started working at the age of fourteen, I never went again until I was in my late twenties), and all kinds of neat stuff like that.

Then it happened, the one day I tried to forget about for years—the day I used alcohol and drugs to help erase it from my life, the day God gave me the strength to overcome. That day changed my life and how I felt for an exceptionally long time. I had stayed over at their house many times, but that night, this so-called friend, the one my age and the one I got closest to, showed his authentic self to me by raping me. I lay there not moving because I did not know what to do, and he said not to tell anyone. I did not tell anyone for years, until I was in rehab, what he did. He did touch me one more time, which I believe was because I did not tell anyone, and he tried a couple more times after that, but I would not allow him to.

I thought if I told anyone about what he did, they would hate me, and I would lose the only male friends I had, but let me tell you something: No violation of this kind is worth keeping a secret! It is cancer in itself because it will eat at you and eat at you until you speak it out and know that it is nothing you did. If I said something, they would think I did something to provoke it, a lie from the pit of hell! I was only a friend to a friend, and that friend violated the friendship. This is just how the devil wants us to act, to feel bad because of the action someone else did, to keep quiet because no one will believe you, and by the way, you committed a sin, so just keep doing it.

After that time, I was not the same, and as time passed, I stopped going over there. I would only go around to see my dad number 2, and sometimes to see how everyone was doing. After he moved out, I would go over a little more, but that grew old since there was no one to hang out with. By the time this was all taking place, I started working on the farm during the summer and finding other things to do the rest of the time.

This became part of my past that stood in the way of my future and was another block to a wall that held me back from achieving my best.

There is so much more I could write about, how empty my life was and how boring it was for me, how I went to electronics school, and how when I graduated, everywhere I went for a job said I did not have enough experience, and finally, I just gave up. It was no wonder that when I got a girl pregnant at the age of twenty-four, I ran from my responsibilities and could not be a father to my son. I was not whole. I know that I could stay in this chapter and give you my whole life history, but that is not what this book is about. I only wanted to provide some highlights so you can see where I came from. You can see through many years of a dysfunctional life that I was on an emotional roller coaster ride: not a fun place to be when you are living it, and I am so glad I no longer have a ticket.

As I wrote this chapter, I saw that there was so much of my life that was influenced by the choices I made:

- ✝ rejection
- ✝ bitterness
- ✝ resentment
- ✝ hurt
- ✝ lack
- ✝ anger (which is only the cover of lies inside)
- ✝ loneliness
- ✝ hopelessness
- ✝ shame
- ✝ abandonment
- ✝ disappointment

And as I got older, it just built to the point that I started to look in other areas for something to fill the void. I wish I knew back then that not knowing Jesus is that void! I would not have gone through all those years feeling empty.

In the following chapter, I will share some of the dreams and goals I had during those times of loneliness.

Chapter 2

Dreams, Visions, and Goals

I want to start this chapter by giving Webster's Dictionary's meanings of dreams, visions, and goals.[6]

Dream (dreamed or dreamt [dremt], dream-ing) as a noun means the following:

1. a succession of images, thoughts, or emotions occurring during sleep
2. a daydream or reverie
3. a goal or aim
4. a wild fancy
5. something of unreal beauty

As an intransitive verb, the word *dream* means the following:

6. to have dreams
7. to indulge in daydreams
8. to conceive of something remotely

As a transitive verb, *dream* means the following:

9. to have a dream of
10. to pass or spend (time) in dreaming
11. dream up, Informal, to devise or concoct

How many of these fit you? For me, it could be all eleven meanings.

Vision (vizh'en) as a noun means the following:

1. the act or power of seeing
2. unusual foresight
3. an image or idea of a spiritual nature seen or obtained under the influence of a divine or other agency
4. an imaginative conception or anticipation
5. a person or thing of extraordinary beauty

I will take number four for my youth and numbers three and four for now.

Goal (gol) as a noun means the following:

1. the result toward which effort is directed
2. the terminal point in a race
3. a place toward or into which players of various sports must drive an object to score
4. the score thus made

As you can see, there is more to dreams than visions and goals. It is okay to be a dreamer as long as you put a plan toward an idea and then reach the goal! This is something for most of my life I did not do! I know God's word says, "Then the Lord answered me and said: Write the vision and make it plain on tablets, that he may run who reads it" (Habakkuk 2:2).

So if you are going to dream, put it into a vision, write it, and then aim for the goal, and do not stop until you get there.

In this chapter, I will share some of my dreams, visions, and goals as a young boy and even as a young man (not in any timeline order). Some came to pass, and some were destroyed by a mindset of stinking thinking, some from drinking and drugging, and some from my past hurt.

As you read this, I want you to see that I was a normal kid. But with the way my youth was, I had no one to help guide me and show me that there is always a way, no matter what family you were born into and how poor they were. Some of the most remarkable men and women we see are poor; they just learned how to overcome obstacles.

Sometimes, a person has enough strength to overcome, and sometimes, we fall into a vast pit, and after we scrape our way close to the top, we hope to make it out, even if it is just a little hope. Then something hits us to knock us back down. There is no set number of times this would happen to a person before they lose that hope and just sit down to give up.

This is when hopelessness, fear that none of your dreams will ever come to pass, depression, a "who cares" attitude, "Why should I bother? I will never get out of here anyway" mindset will knock you down every time. And when you lose hope, you feel like your life is empty and means nothing.

I know; I have been there!

You know what? I still can feel that way today, sometimes all day long. The difference between then and now is that I have a relationship with someone who speaks positive things into my life.

> You can do it. Never give up. It is about to change. It is not about when you will meet your dreams. It is about reaching for your goals and keeping them in sight. Then the manifestation has the power to develop. (JC)

In the first chapter, I shared about my neighbor (Dad Number 2) who helped me in some ways, like telling me to finish school, but I think by the time he came into my life, there was so much hurt that I never realized I could have taken all he had to give and use it to overcome a lot of those obstacles. I hope you have someone like this in your life because I am here to tell you to stop and listen to them, just as if you were crossing a railroad track. You would see the sign and obey it; I hope you would stop, look, and listen to see if a train is coming. If you do not have someone, I pray right now that God will send someone into your life.

Okay, within the following few pages, I will share some of my dreams, visions, and goals. Remember, I did not have what I just shared with you to set the course of my life, so if you see some goals I did not hit, learn from them, and do not make the same mistakes I did. My goal for this book is to help you see more clearly.

When I was a young boy, I think I had all the same dreams little boys have, like being a doctor, veterinarian, ballplayer, teacher, policeman, astronaut, architect, etcetera. But then, as I grew older, I started to have other dreams, some of which were way out of my reach, and they never went anywhere. But some of them were within distance if I wanted to go after them, like learning how to play an instrument, read music, being in a band, being a weatherman, being a truck driver like my dad, being a good husband and dad, and being a TV producer/cameraman, singer, train engineer, etcetera.

I did get to operate a train once with friends from one of the home bars I hung out at. They were from Pennsylvania but had worked in our town for years with the local railroad. They invited me one Saturday to go with them to deliver some paper material to a neighboring city. So as we started, they asked me if I wanted to operate it, and of course, I said yes. So I jumped in the chair, threw the engineer's hat on, and then they demonstrated how to operate the controls. It was awesome. I almost peed my pants!

One of the most incredible things I learned in the last twenty-two years was that no dream, vision, or goal is out of reach. As long as you keep your focus up and your knees down on the ground, anything is possible to those in Christ Jesus (see Mark 9:23, 10:27). I will show you how this worked for me in a later chapter.

Being the youngest child, on any road trips my parents did take to see family, I would most likely be the only one with them. Because they were not good communicators, there was not much talking during those trips. This gave me much time to stare out the window and think. This opened the door to loneliness. I dreamed of being an astronaut as I looked at the sky. In 1969, when *Apollo 11* landed on the moon and Neil Armstrong took the first step, I was glued to the TV set. For hours, I would watch anything about it, and I started to cut all the articles from the newspaper and made my scrapbook, which I kept for many years. I would read about it, and then one day, I learned what was needed to be an astronaut—college and lots of it. Knowing my dad would never be able to send me, I stopped dreaming of going to the moon after a couple of years.

Also, I used to look out at the sky and wonder how the weather worked. So when I got into high school, one of my science teachers had a weather setup in his class, and he would teach all about the weather and how it worked. So I joined his class and started to learn about the clouds and their names, do not ask me to name them; that was a long time ago, and all the tools of the trade. I would even go to the primary office every morning and give our weather report over the PA system. I loved it so much that I thought I might attend college after high school to be a weatherman or storm chaser.

I would sit on the porch during storms to see how they moved and how lightning would work. To see what type of storm the violent atmospheric disturbance developed into. The following year, I did not get to take that class, and the interest faded even though I still get amazed at how the weather works, and I still like to sit out during storms, especially lightning storms. I love storms; I do not like the destruction that comes with them, but I like how they form.

When I lived in Texas, we had threats of tornadoes from time to time, and one night, I went to my son's karate class when the pastor came to the instructor to warn him that the church was in the line of a tornado. Want to know what I did? I ran outside to see it; I had to. I waited all my life to see one up close and personal. Well, I pulled out my phone and started to video its approach until it was right over the top of me, blowing me around, and dirt hitting me in the face like I was in a sandblaster. My ex-wife yelled for me to come in, but I was so intrigued that I had to stay out.

I will say that if I felt like my life was in any immediate danger, I would have gone in. Sometimes you can teach a boy how to be a man, but you cannot take the boy out of the man.

In the first chapter, I mentioned going with my dad on a few road trips and said I would tell you about one of those trips, so here it goes.

The truck my dad drove was an eighteen-wheel gasoline tanker; he would go to Philadelphia, Pennsylvania, to fill it up at a refinery and then deliver the gas to whatever station was on his list. He may do anywhere from four to maybe six loads a day. Well, I was about eight years old on this one trip, and we were going over the bridge from New Jersey and had to cross the Delaware River. Just as we were getting to the top at the halfway mark, the air brake lines blew, and we had no brakes. My dad was an excellent driver, and this day, to me, put him at the top. He thought quickly and knew that if he kept going and we started on the downside of the bridge, there was no stopping that tanker.

So you know what he did. He stopped, put his hazards on, and started going backward. With my heart pumping away, I watched in the review mirror and saw cars closing in on us, slowing down, and then going around us. After about forty-five minutes, we made it off the bridge and into what used to be a guardhouse at the foot of the bridge. He then got out and went to call his boss; we did not have cell phones back then. I was so impressed with that trip that I still tell truck drivers that story.

So, as I grew and was looking at what I wanted to do with my life, I was as normal as any other boy; I wanted to be a truck driver like my dad. I told my dad, who answered me by saying, "You do not want to drive trucks, kid. It is a hard life, and you will never make anything of it! Look at me; no pay and many hours!"

I did listen to my dad and never drove as a profession, but I did learn to drive and had my time driving a big rig or any type of truck, especially when I started to work on the farm. Whenever I drove a truck, I would think of my dad and how good it made me feel doing what he did all his life.

Also, in the first chapter, I told you about when I would go with my dad to my uncle's house and play the piano. I dreamt of being a prominent pianist playing all the big stages with all the big names. I would tell my dad and mom I wanted to take lessons, but there was no way they would be able to pay for them. My uncle even mentioned he would pay for them, but my parents would not allow it. So again, I had to take a dream and throw it away because my parents were poor.

However, in sixth grade, I had an opportunity to join the school band, so my mom took me to the meeting and worked out a way to get a trumpet. I was so excited! I was finally going to learn how to read music and play an instrument. I could not stop talking about it! I remember running to lessons, excited that I had found something I could call my own!

Then one day, I was not feeling too good. My stomach was hurting badly, and my mom had to take me to the doctor. After he checked me out, he told my mom she had to get me to the hospital immediately because my appendix was about to explode. No problem; I have been in the hospital for my tonsils, all the ice cream I could eat, and gifts. So away we go!

After the operation and getting close to being released, I found out that it would be six weeks before I could return to school. Hooray! No Sister Mary for a while, who was my teacher, and I was always in trouble with her. Even though she did visit me in the hospital, it would be nice to be away from her. So, to the point of the story, since I would be away from school for so long, I would not be able to attend band practice.

I tried to practice at home, but because of the surgery, it hurt too much. So by the time I got back to school, I was so far behind in class. There goes another vision because of stinking thinking. I know today that if I wanted to, I would have been able to get caught up with the rest of the class with much hard work, but because of the lack of support to guide me, I never tried.

If you are in something like this, I am here to tell you that if you want to complete what you are doing badly enough, you can do it! There is help; it is called prayer.

I learned to play the guitar a little bit from a friend (I will talk about him in the next chapter), who gave me a white Gibson and an amplifier. I would sit in my bedroom for hours, trying to play and sing and write songs. I never did get any good at it. Neighbors tell me to stop singing and keep the guitar down. Hey, it is not that I cannot sing; it was the amplifier.

When I got to high school, I joined the choir. I remember the first day walking into the classroom and the teacher asking me if he could help me, and I said, "I am here to join the class."

He said, "We have another bass, everyone."

It made me feel welcomed, as if I belonged to something. So I put a lot into it and enjoyed it. We sang concerts at school and even went on the road a few times. Christmas was the best with all the good, cheerful songs to sing like "Joy to the World," "Little Town of Bethlehem," and, my favorite, "Silent Night." If you know the song, stop to sing it and listen to the words. Thank God for his love.

"For God so loved the world that He gave His only begotten Son, that whoever believes in Him should not perish but have everlasting life" (John 3:16).

Okay, let us get back to the stories.

When I was around nine years old, I got a slide projector as a gift, and I thought maybe I could use it to make some money. Since some of the kids I knew did not get to go to the movie theater, I set up a movie theater in the basement. I used a sheet for the screen and put chairs in a row, just like you would see in a theater. I handed out flyers that looked something like this:

Anthony's Movie Theater
Starring Mickey Mouse
Saturday: 1:00 p.m.

All seats are 10 cents.
Popcorn for a Nickel

It was fantastic that first Saturday to see about twelve kids show up. I made almost two dollars on my first showing and started to make a list of what I was going to buy. Then my mom started to get phone calls from the kids' parents complaining that her son had taken money from their kids. I had to give it all back.

This started an entrepreneurial spirit that instantly robbed me of growth. I went through many different things with the expectation that I would have to return the money. I say it this way to show that words and actions can create walls in our thoughts.

Remember me telling you in the first chapter about our house? I want to share a little more about it. I loved that house so much that I used to dream about it day and night about how I could upgrade it and make it bigger. I wanted to change the landscape and add a garage and workshop in the back because I love to work on woodworking. You see, it was falling apart—the plaster on the walls and ceilings was cracking, the doors were old, creaky, and drafty, and the basement had a dirt floor with a giant coal heater that looked like an octopus with all of its duck work going all over the place. I dug pieces of coal out of that floor for years. It had wood siding with hardly any paint and old, drafty windows.

It was like something you would see in a western movie. Get the picture?

Oh, one more funny story; during the winter, when it got cold and windy, my dad would use newspaper to fill the cracks in the front door so the snow would not blow in. And my mom would put up a blanket between the living and dining rooms to keep the heat in one room. Yes, the living room was off-limits unless you wanted to put on the snowsuit because it was so cold that the steam would come out of your mouth.

One night, I had a dream: I took the roof off and made it higher so we could use the attic, and I added an elevator to go from the basement to the attic; I even drew up plans. I started to work on it as I got older, having my dad pay for the materials, and I did the labor with my brother, helping out sometimes until he left for the Air Force. The biggest thing I did before taking ownership was to rewire the whole house; it needed it in the worst way. I remember my mom telling my dad she smelled wires burning. At first, he would go around looking; then, after a bunch of times, he would just keep sitting in his chair.

Well, she was right. She did smell wires burning.

When I took ownership of that house, I fulfilled that dream minus the elevator. I took the roof entirely off to add a third floor. It took ten days to complete that job, and I only had one rainstorm. Thank God I had found a super large tarp to keep it covered. We built a 24' × 40' three-car garage, which was big enough to put a workshop in. And I redid the landscape with underground irrigation.

I do miss that old house; I put a lot of sweat and tears into it. I should never have sold it.

As I write this chapter, I am getting many memories of things I used to dream about, but for the sake of time, I am only picking the most important ones.

Hey, how about this one? I wanted to be a millionaire. Is this one original? I do not think so, right? Every poor kid dreams of being a millionaire, but only a few make it. I made it! I am waiting for the bank to transfer the cash into my account.

No, I am just kidding. I would love to be a one-percenter in this natural world, and maybe I will be, as long as I stay focused on the scripture, "Greater is he who is in me than he that is in this world" (1 John 4:4).

I will end this chapter with one big dream I had because it shows how powerful negative thoughts and feelings can be. They can alter your life and put you on a road you did not intend to travel. I was getting ready to graduate from high school, and the guidance office asked me if I knew what I would do with my life.

I gave it some thought and spent some time looking at different brochures. I decided to follow a dream I had for a long time—a TV Producer/cameraman or something in the field. In high school, I joined the audio/visual group and did a lot of stage work, running cameras, setting up lights, and working on sound. I became vice president of the Audio-Visual Club and was given the audiovisual award called the King's Picture Award. This was all before I started to head in the wrong direction; my head was still clear, and I knew what I wanted from my life, at least I thought so.

So I went into the guidance office and told them what I wanted to do, and the next step came. One big step, I felt like Neil Armstrong when he walked on the moon, having to find a college, and apply. I found one of the top five colleges at that time for TV production, Boston University, and I was so excited that I could not stop talking about it.

I was finally going to do something with my life and not be like my parents, enjoy what I am doing, and make money. That day was one of my life's most significant, profound, darkest days. I remember sitting there in the guidance office filling out the forms, and when the question "How much do your parents earn a year?" came up, I sat there for a few minutes and was ready to cry.

Thinking this is it, because my parents are poor, again, I am not going to be able to do something, not realizing at the time that us being poor could have been a good thing for grants or scholarships. But, with anger, I tore up the forms, threw them in the trash, and ran out of that place fast. I do not remember exactly where I ran to; I just remember not wanting to go home because the shame was so great.

I never did make it to college then; I just used it as another stepping-stone toward the bottom of the pit I was getting accustomed to. King Baby does not get what he wants, so he cries and runs to hide. That is me, which is what I was famous for. Is that pathetic, or what? If you have never heard this before, the King Baby Syndrome is, "I want what I want, and I want it now."

I would hope that so far, with these first two chapters, you can see how my life up to this point was somewhat normal. You might be saying, "Heck, this guy's life was a piece of cake compared to mine," and you might be right. I am trying to lay the foundation that no matter who you are, or where you may come from, there is a stronghold that can take hold of anyone with weak spots.

My weak spot was more on the pain I felt and how I made a mountain out of a molehill than the family I was born into. A minor dysfunction goes a long way when you do not know how to be an overcomer or are taught how to deal with issues.

Chapter 3

How It All Started

Now that I told you a little about my youth, I would like to share how the addiction almost destroyed my life.

Webster's Dictionary[7] says that *addict* means:

1. a person who is addicted: a *drug addict* (v. t) to give (oneself) up to something habitually To cause (a person) to depend physiologically on a drug

Merriam-Webster online dictionary[8] says:

Definition of *Addict*

1. one exhibiting a compulsive, chronic, physiological, or psychological need for a habit-forming substance, behavior, or activity
2. one strongly inclined to do, use, or indulge in something repeatedly

Definition of *Addiction*

1. a compulsive, chronic, physiological, or psychological need for a habit-forming substance, behavior, or activity having harmful

physical, psychological, or social effects and typically causing well-defined symptoms (such as anxiety, irritability, tremors, or nausea) upon withdrawal or abstinence: the state of being addicted. i.e., alcohol addiction, an addiction to prescription painkillers, drug addictions, and gambling addiction
2. a strong inclination to do, use, or indulge in something repeatedly

Addictions can be Substances, Impulse Control Disorders, and Behavioral, including but not limited to alcohol abuse, drug abuse, exercise abuse, pornography, shopping, and gambling. Classic hallmarks of addiction include: impaired control over substances/behavior, preoccupation with substance/behavior, continued use despite consequences, and denial. Habits and patterns associated with addiction are typically characterized by immediate gratification (short-term reward) and delayed deleterious effects (long-term costs). Physiological dependence occurs when the body has to adjust to the substance by incorporating the substance into its 'normal' functioning. This state creates the conditions of tolerance and withdrawal.

Tolerance is the process by which the body continually adapts to the substance and requires increasingly more significant amounts to achieve the original effects.

Withdrawal refers to physical and psychological symptoms people experience when reducing or discontinuing a substance the body has become dependent on. Symptoms of withdrawal generally include, but are not limited to, anxiety, irritability, intense cravings for the substance, nausea, hallucinations, headaches, cold sweats, and tremors.

In chapter 1, I mentioned that my parents were not drinkers. The only thing close to addiction was that my dad smoked cigarettes almost his whole life, and my mom was addicted to church. So I did not inherit the drug and alcohol addiction; it came through the back door of pain, emotions, and hurts.

Remember, I said that the saying, "Sticks and stones may hurt me, but words will never harm me," was wrong? Well, I can prove it in my life as well as in the Word of God. It is sneaky, slow, like a roller coaster ride. When you first start, you see that you are moving, you hear the chain clanging, and then you hit the curve at the top and take the plunge down as fast as possible. Life can be this way; one day, you are playing with army men, then your surroundings are playing with your emotions. You hit a curve in the highway to find yourself plunging so fast that even if you want to, you cannot stop until you hit bottom.

I know that my life was not a big mess, like some people, but by the time my teenage years were done, there was a complete 180-degree turn from when I turned fifteen. This lasted from 1973 to October 5, 1989.

I also mentioned in chapter 1 that I loved being by my mom's side. When I turned thirteen, I was still under my mom's shadow. I wanted to go wherever she went and did not care what anyone said, so the family moved in across the street. Within three years, I started to leave my mother's side and take on the image of what I should be doing. I was beginning to become a man. I was starting to rebel; I did not call it that back then. That is when all the hurt from my neighbor, the lack of physical love from my family, and all those emotions built up over the years started to erupt.

I wanted to be a grown-up teen but did not know how to maneuver through the emotions I was feeling, the lack of a dad around, and my brothers' not knowing how to be big brothers to me. I was heading for that curve on the highway. Even though my brothers would not let me hang out with them, I still wanted to be like them, just like any little brother. It did not matter that they did not care to have me around most of the time. I think that is why I was so attracted to the boys across the street.

At this time, I had a taste of my first beer. I was fifteen years old when I was at the neighbor's house one day after school. We went downstairs to the basement and raided the refrigerator, and what I remember about the taste is that it was nice and cold and went down easily. After the first three bottles, I felt funny, and my vision was cloudy. Then, after a few more, I felt no fear about anything.

One of the guys there lived downtown, so we rode our bicycles to his house. I was laughing like no other time and had difficulty keeping the bike straight, almost getting hit by some passing cars. After we got there, we went to the second floor of the garage, and it was not that long before I felt sick and vomited all over the father's truck through a hole in the floor. I swore I would never touch a beer again.

Would you like me to show how strong willpower is?

I was in high school and had to walk to school because we lived too close for me to take the bus. One day after school, my brother asked me if I needed a ride home. I do not need to tell you how long I had to think about that answer! He had a '98 Oldsmobile, and to me, it was fantastic to have the opportunity to ride in it.

One day, as we were going down the road, I saw him pull something out of his cigarette box and light it. It did not look like a cigarette and did not smell like it either. Then he handed it to me and said to take a hit. I asked him what it was, and he said it was a joint that would make me feel better. It choked me, and I felt funny after a few more hits. When I got home, I went to my bedroom, lay on my bed, and noticed that it was not so bad. That became a habit with him picking me up from school for a while, and soon enough, I was looking into getting my own.

I have to make sure you understand I am not putting any blame on my brother for the path I took. I had a choice that first time, and I chose to take the destructive one. One of the main parts of our life is to accept our responsibility. So if you are blaming someone else for your mistakes, please try to learn about this so you can be set free.

As I was getting high, I noticed that the pain I felt as a young kid was starting to be replaced with a different feeling that did not hurt. When I asked about this feeling, I was told it is because it makes everything easier to cope with. Folks, this is a huge lie, and it is a shame that many people believe it; I am glad I am no longer one.

AN INJECTION OF FAITH

So I started to wonder, *If what they are telling me is true, how would it make me feel if I were to do more than just smoke weed?* So I started to drink some wine with classmates during school dances. This made me so sick that at one of the dances, I made a fool of myself, and I got sick all over the floor and cussed out one of the teachers, so she called the police. When the officer came, he took me to the station and called my parents. My father did not say too much, but my mother was mad. I think she did not understand what was going on. She was more concerned with people finding out that it would make her look. She always said that if a policeman ever escorted me home, she would beat me back to tomorrow.

I had been working on the farm, and summer was coming around, so that meant I would be working long days, six to seven days a week, for about three months. This was when other drugs started to be introduced to me, drugs that would help me to stay up longer and work more without being tired—drugs like cocaine and black beauties (a.k.a. speed), that, as long as you keep taking them, they will not make you sick. It is called crashing, coming down, hitting your low, and whatever else you may know it as.

I started to buy weed by the pound, pills by the bag, and cocaine by the ounce; this is outside what was given to me for free. Most of the guys were doing it; when one person did not have some, someone else did. I did this for years; it was the only way I could have done those long hours on the farm. There was a time when getting the drugs was difficult, so a friend of mine and myself would stop at a hobby shop to buy model glue, cut it open, and throw it in a paper bag so we could huff it. It would make us lightheaded and was an excellent substitute for drugs. Wow! I wonder how many brain cells I killed with that stuff!

When I got to the point where I wanted more and could not afford it, I started to sell them. I never made any money because I would consume more than I sold, and sometimes, I did not sell any of it. I would just keep it for myself. After years of doing this, one time, one of my connections sent a hit man after me to break my legs if I did not pay up. I worked out a deal with the man and am still walking. That is when I started to notice I was having a problem.

This next section has a long history in my life, so I will not spend much time elaborating on it because it would be a book. I want you to see how you can take a dream from your youth, and because you want it so bad, you will go to any lengths to make it come to pass.

I told you in the second chapter about some of my dreams, and one of them was to be in a band. Since I never finished learning how to play an instrument back in grade school, I did not think this would come to pass, but it did! I hooked up with some guys from my school who formed a rock 'n' roll band and started to play at school dances, and they needed some help. I do not recall precisely how I came to join them, but I began to go around with them to hook up wires and carry equipment in and out of the truck, and then I started working the lights/soundboard when they would play.

They started playing at other functions like parties, weddings, and bars, which was beginning to get exciting. There was a song for this part of life, "Sex, Drugs and Rock 'n' Roll." Initially, it was not at a fast pace, but after the word got around on how good they were, they started getting phone calls for gigs. I loved it and could not wait for the end of the week because most of them were on the weekends.

I believe that I enjoyed this lifestyle because the whole time I was with them, I was not thinking about how sad I felt about my past. I spent much time with these guys during those years, not just playing gigs, but doing things like winter/summer bowling leagues and sometimes just hanging out. As time passed, the band members went in different directions, and one of the guitar players looked into hooking up with some other guys who would write original music. Because I felt close to this person, I went with him, which took me to a new level.

This is the same person who gave me the first guitar I spoke about in the second chapter, and the one friend I still had through most of my life until I found God and had to walk away from him and his wife in fear of being told to get lost. Not because of the people, places, and things you learn in the twelve-step programs, but because he supported me during those years. I will share why I just said this in chapter 10. We would go to the Philadelphia area for practice, and this would be during the week, and then we would have gigs on the weekend, sometimes in other states. This was nothing but a big party, getting high all the time and playing at nightclubs for all the free beer we could drink. "This is the life," that is what I used to say.

My official title was a roadie. I even have my name on a vinyl album, a.k.a. record, titled "911"[9]; see pic in back. (For all of you who do not know what a record is, it is a large, black, round disk, twelve inches in diameter, that we listen to music on with a needle.) I did not join a band playing an instrument, but to me, this was just as good; it was a fast-paced, exciting, out-of-this-world experience, and I loved it!

Between that first joint and the time with the band 911, I had a series of different people I would hang with to get high at every chance. Sometimes, they used me, and other times, I used them to find that so-called peace in our lives we were searching for. It was within this time that I started to let my hair grow longer. It was past my shoulder blades when I had it cut. My dad used to tell me I looked like a...Well, I cannot say it; just let your imagination ride with this one. This would all be the tail end of high school through vocational-technical school and the trying to find myself era that took me to my mid-twenties.

I am unsure about the year the band stopped playing; I know it was at least 1985. I saw all the guys when we all got together for the Super Bowl party we had every year. Even when I got clean, I would go, but it was not a good place for me.

Then there was a time in my life when I was doing the Nightclub scene without the band. I lived on the East Coast, only thirty-four miles from the Atlantic Ocean. There were club strips in Margate that would be open on Friday and Saturday nights, and when the band was not playing, and even after the band broke up, I would go there until they closed. I would also hit the bars in between on many of those weekends. Now, the bars were becoming a significant source of my highs.

I started a job with a plumbing company, and the one owner would hang out at the bar in whatever area we worked in. In most cases, we would meet him after we were done with work, and I would end up staying almost all night. The other owner lived on top of a bar, which would also be a big hangout for me, especially when my brother started to bartend, and when I did not have any money, he would give me a few dollars.

Sometimes I would wake up, sometimes the next day, and the first thing I would do was look out the window to see if my car was out there. I later discovered that what I was experiencing was called a blackout—temporary unconsciousness. Wow! I had many of those in those days; I hope I never harmed anyone driving home.

I was going over the names of the clubs and bars I used to go to, and as I was going through them, I realized there were too many to name, so the closest number I came up with was seventy-five different bars/clubs from 1976 to 1989 when I went to rehab. Some of them became home bars for years. I even bartended at one so that I could drink for free.

I started to play pool and got incredibly good at the game. Many days, I would go to the bar and play for drinks, and by the end of the night, I would have a stack of markers for free drinks, which most of the time I would give away, and the only money I spent was on the pool table. I joined the pool league just so I could be with the in-crowd, and I also joined the local bar horseshoe team. One of the main parts of the tournaments was drinking and smoking weed.

As you can see, everything I was involved in had something to do with alcohol or drugs; anything else was not worth my time. This became my life; I believed everything was fine, and this would be just how I was. No big deal, right? Keep Reading.

Chapter 4

Going Against the Current!

The Bible tells us how we are to live our lives. Since I went to a Catholic school for eight years, kindergarten through sixth grade (repeating the third grade), and was an altar boy for around two of those years, God was trying to set my course in the right direction. Instead of following the path he had for me, I became rebellious to my family, not only to my parents and life in general but to God Himself.

I was not the perfect student in grade school and would be in trouble from time to time, which would lead to getting sent to the hallway so everyone walking by would know I did something wrong, or getting sent to the office, or having to write something like "I will not talk in class" one thousand times, or asked to come up front and put my hand on the desk with my knuckles up so I could get the yardstick across them—that hurt! Can you imagine what names I called those nuns?

I remember one nun telling me that God had a chalkboard in heaven with my name on it, and every time I was terrible, an angel would put a mark on it, and when it was filled, I would go to hell. It must be a large board; I am still here. As a young boy of ten years of age,

I no longer cared about what God's plan was. I just knew that if this is how God works, I do not want anything to do with Him! That is when I turned away from religion and wanted nothing to do with it.

The name of this chapter, *"Going Against the Current,"* is because of my choice to turn from God and do things my way.

As I shared with you in the last chapter, I believed everything was fine with my life, even though I was drinking, smoking weed, doing cocaine, or speeding. At least I was not shooting anything up my veins. I made it a point not to go there because I have been with others and even helped some people shoot up, and I wouldn't say I liked how it made their eyes roll back in their heads, then drop to the floor, passing out. Sometimes, I would have to smack them to come out of it. This did not seem fun to me.

I thought this was the way it was going to be. I know this was not the way I dreamed my life to be, as I shared with you in the first chapters, but it was the way the current of life was taking me. I was seeing that I was having a hard time keeping friends because the only thing that mattered was me, and if it was not going that way, I would be nasty and mean, making people leave our friendship.

I remembered one time in 1979, I had a girl who started to talk to me at one of the bars, and for weeks, she would be wherever I was. Sometimes, she would go to my house late at night and sit outside waiting for me to come home, sometimes until 3:00 to 4:00 in the morning. She was a beautiful girl, and I liked her. My only problem was that she was too hyper, and I could not deal with that personality. I also did not get along with her brothers, which did not help. So I told her I did not want anything to do with her, only to find out weeks later that she was pregnant, and at first, I did not think the baby was mine. But after he was born on March 18, 1980, and when I saw him, I knew that this beautiful baby was mine.

I am not sure what transpired that day; I just knew I did not want his mom, and it was something like, if I did not take her, I could not see my boy. That is what she told me. This was stinking thinking because I just dropped it and continued with my life.

After I ended the relationship, I went about my own business, building on my addiction and doing my own thing until I met someone I fell in love with; well, I thought it was love. So that Christmas, I asked her to marry me. This marked the second most important day of my life! At least, that is what it looked like. That February, we found out she was pregnant, so we pushed up the wedding so the baby would not be considered illegitimate. I wanted to do something right for a change. On August 2, 1982, she went into labor, so I drove her to the hospital, and even though she was not ready then, they kept her because it was six weeks early.

I got tired of sitting around, not having anything to drink or drugs, so I went out to my car and got high. Being self-centered caused me to forget why I was there until there was a nudge that felt to go in. When I got upstairs, I heard a nurse calling my name and saying my wife was ready to go into labor. They threw a gown on me, and in I went. After a few minutes, the doctor came in, and there I was, on August 3, 1982, at 1:33 a.m., right alongside him, watching my baby girl being born with emotions flying all over the place in a buzzing way.

They carted her off and put her in an incubator because she was only 4 pounds, 8 ounces, and I realized that because of my addiction, I almost missed the third most important day in my life. I was going to quit, at least try to, but as you will see later, it never happened.

When that beautiful little girl turned five, I was by myself again. Her mom could not take my drinking and drugging anymore, so she decided to leave one day. She gave the baby to the grandmother and proceeded to live her own life. Because of how it turned out with my son, I would not let that happen again, not that my son was no less important to me. I just had a better chance with my daughter. So I fought with the grandparents until they gave her back to me.

It started great with my mom's help until I took her to the bars with me, sometimes until early in the morning. I am not proud of this and almost did not put it in the book, but I needed to, so I could show how bad the addiction was starting to be. I was not thinking straight. I was turning to the love of my life, drugs, alcohol, smoking dope, etcetera, instead of focusing on what counted—my loving daughter. Praise God, she does not hold that time against me.

Then one day, her other grandmother came to take her for a visit and never returned her home because they believed it was for the best. Of course, I disagreed with them, but they would not budge from their decision.

Because of everything going wrong in my life, I decided to leave town with the carnival. *Yes, I said carnival!* A friend of mine was one of the sons of a five-brother large carnival company that ran the East Coast, the "Amusements of America." Every year, from fourteen until twenty-seven, I would work a sideshow or a game, and since there was nothing for me in Hammonton, New Jersey, at least, I thought, I decided to go on the road with them. We worked our way up the coast to Canada and then backed down to finish the season in Macon, Georgia; I even got to drive an eighteen-wheeler. The only time I went back home was for court because, just before leaving, I was at the carnival grounds partying all night and smashed up the car the following day.

While writing this, I stopped for a few minutes to remember all the accidents and how many cars I had totaled. I came up with about ten accidents and four vehicles totaled. I was making some bad mistakes.

Well, my life was nothing but bad decisions at that point anyway, drinking every night after work until the bars closed in every town we went to, smoking pot during the day, and doing cocaine when possible, as well as smoking it. I was so afraid of getting my butt kicked that I found the most prominent man on the lot and made friends with him. He worked the big wheel, and I could ride the rides any time I wanted, so I would go there and ask him if he wanted to get high. This led to a great friendship; no one on the lot would mess with me because of him. And even if a local person from whatever town we were in started with me, he would stand between us, so I never had to worry about getting beaten up.

About one month on the road, I met another girl whom I started to date, and after the season with the carnival was over, I asked her to come home with me. She was a lovely girl who ran away from home, and I thought maybe I could help her get her life together. (Isn't that just like an addict? Assuming you can help other people with their lives when your own life is going down the tubes!)

It was great in the beginning; I went to my daughter's grandparents to see if I could get her back, and after they saw that my life was different and that there was a girl in my life to help raise her, they gave her back.

Everything was fair those first few years, my relationship with my girlfriend seemed stable, and I had a hold on my drinking and drugging.

To add to my blessing, one day at the local carnival, my son's uncle, whom he was living with, came up to me and asked if I wanted to meet my son. Of course, I said yes with excitement! I remember he was in his uncle's arms, and every time I looked at him, he would turn to the other side. After some time had passed, we started to build on our relationship.

I asked him how he liked the gifts I sent him, and he said he never got any from me. I was not happy with that because I used to go to a bar where his grandmother would visit, and I would give her gifts to give to him for his birthday and Christmas. Here, she never gave them to him from me; she would change the tag. I was so mad when he told me that!

I took him to Little League, coached third base, went fishing and camping, and even got to have him sleep overnight one Christmas, one of the most important days of the year, when I got to wake up with my son and daughter under the tree. Wow! My emotions were all over the place that day. I loved it! But after his mom heard about our relationship, she came to New Jersey and took him back to Missouri with her. The next time I saw him, he was around twenty when he returned to New Jersey for a visit.

Then, one New Year's Eve, I did not feel like going to the bar to party, so my girlfriend went out alone. She never came home until the following day, hungover, tired, and with her stockings torn up, and I knew what she had done.

After this, I was not the same and started to go deeper into my addiction. I would drink more and could not get enough drugs to bury the pain. Remember in chapter 1 that I mentioned the Dago Red my dad drank? That wine became one of my favorites, and I could not get enough of it. Shortly after this, I started to shoot up. Remember earlier in the chapter when I said this was something I would never do? Well, I lied to myself. It became a new high, a new way of life, and a new path of destruction. I kept this up until I hit my bottom. I will explain this in the next chapter.

It is so true what they say about addiction. It never goes backward; it keeps going deeper and deeper into your soul, where it plays with the mind, will, and emotions. I thought I had everything under control, but the addiction had me under its control. It told me where it wanted me to go, what it wanted me to do, how to do it, and whom to do it with.

As you were reading this chapter, did you see the pattern? I did! I did not realize until now how bad it was. I have to be in a relationship, afraid to be alone. Do you think it was because of my lack of love as a kid, and I felt a girl would fill the void? I think so!

These are the health risks associated with using illegal drugs and alcohol. Some of the significant dangers I found on the National Institute on Drug Abuse (NIH)[10] website;

- ✓ *Alcohol:* Increased risk of injuries, violence, fetal damage (in pregnant women); depression; neurologic deficits; hypertension; liver and heart disease; addiction; fatal overdose. Marijuana: Cough, frequent respiratory infections; possible mental health decline; addiction.

- ✓ *Heroin:* Constipation; endocarditis; hepatitis; HIV; addiction; fatal overdose.

- ✓ *Cocaine:* Weight loss, insomnia; cardiac or cardiovascular complications; stroke; seizures; addiction, Nasal damage from snorting; Severe dental problems.

- ✓ *Nicotine:* Chronic lung disease; cardiovascular disease; stroke; cancers of the mouth, pharynx, larynx, esophagus, stomach, pancreas, cervix, kidney, bladder, and acute myeloid leukemia; adverse pregnancy outcomes; addiction.

- ✓ *Inhalants: (harmful gases and aerosols, glue, nitrous oxide)* Whippets, poppers, snappers: Most inhalants produce a rapid high that resembles alcohol intoxication. If sufficient amounts are inhaled, nearly all solvents and gases produce a loss of sensation and even unconsciousness. Irreversible effects can be hearing loss, limb spasms, central nervous system or brain damage, or bone marrow damage. Sniffing high concentrations of inhalants may result in death from heart failure or suffocation (inhalants displace oxygen in the lungs).

- ✓ *Hallucinogens: (LSD, PCP, Ecstasy, Mushrooms, etc.)*: Memory loss, difficulties with speech and thinking, depression, weight loss, increased heart rate and blood pressure, tremors, and profound sweating.

Chapter 5

Let Me Out of Here!

This is a short chapter, but it was a massive part of my life and became the turning point that I will always be grateful to God and my family for being there for me.

As I started to say in the last chapter, I was hitting bottom. I was getting so depressed with my life that I wanted out. I walked away from a son, my first marriage turned out to be a waste of time, and the only good thing that came out of it was my daughter. My girlfriend was cheating on me, and only God and she know the number of times. I was spending all of my money in the bars and on drugs; half of the time, I was in la-la land and did not remember one day to the next.

None of my relationships worked, no matter who they were with, and it was hard to cope. The only person who stuck by my side was my mom. She knew something was wrong with me, so she kept praying for me, and even some of the elderly widows I did handyman work for would pray. They would say, "God bless you, kid. You are a good boy."

I could feel a strong presence on me and would have thoughts of how much my mom loved me and conversations with my neighbor Matt (dad number 2). I believe there is power in prayer from someone who loves God and that God hears those prayers and answers them every time.

Today, I am grateful for those prayers. But then, I wanted nothing to do with prayer or what it stood for. I still wanted nothing to do with God and did not care what he thought of me. I was sick and tired of being sick and tired.

I was thirty-two years old with nothing to show for my life but broken hearts, promises, visions, and goals. I was a lousy son, brother, uncle, friend, father, husband, and boyfriend. I did not care about my family; why should I? They were never there for me. I did not care about work. I just wanted to bang on these drums all day and party every night, just like the rock 'n' roll song from Todd Rundgren.

I thought I was a lowlife scumbag. I was ugly from the top of my head to the souls of my feet, and everything inside and around me sounded like a pity party, didn't it? I started not to have a perfect picture of myself, and I just wanted to go to sleep and never get up. The pain was so great that I felt numb and would think of my daughter and how much she needed her father, and that would get another day behind me.

Then one day, my girlfriend left and went back home. I do not remember how many days passed before coming home from partying one night when the bottom hit me. Remember my illustration of a roller coaster ride when you plunge to the bottom after the curve at the top? That is where I was, at the bottom without any hope. I just wanted to sleep and never wake up. This was not the first time I felt like this, but it was this time I reacted to the thoughts that told me it was time to say goodbye.

My niece Kimmy, who was living at the house then, recently told me that when I walked into the house, I approached her when she was lying on the sofa and made an oral sexual advance. She screamed for me to get off and ran out of the room. I sat on the couch for what seemed to be hours, thinking about my life and how messed up it was. That is when I concluded that it was time to go to sleep and never wake up; it was time to end my own life. So I thought to myself, how would I do this, drugs? I did not have enough on me; they weren't the right ones anyway. Jump off the roof? The way my life was going, I probably would only get hurt. Get in the car and crash into something?

Then I remembered something.

When I was in my early twenties, a friend stole a .38 revolver from a house, and I took it from him so he would not get in trouble; little did I know God was going to use this gun as a point of contact. When I took it home that day, it had six bullets in the chamber, and I shot one of them off to see how it felt to shoot it, and then I hid it so no one could find it.

So with excitement, I ran to the shed and dug it out. I sat on the stool and put the gun to my head and thought this is it.

As the tears ran down my face, I pulled the trigger; nothing happened, so I pulled it again. Nothing happened, so I pulled it again, and again, and again, for about five minutes. Even to this day, whenever I think about it, I can still hear the clicking of the trigger, one after the other. I sat there alive and wondered what was going on. I knew when I took this gun home that day that it had six bullets, and I only fired one and then put it away until now. "How could this be! How could this be!" was all I kept saying. I started yelling out to God, "Just let me be! I am tired of this BS and want out! Let me die, please. I can't take this anymore!"

I looked up, and some knives were on my wall with all my tools, so I thought I would use a knife if I could not do it with the gun. I quickly jumped up, grabbed one, and started running it along my wrist. As I said, I wanted this day to be my last. God wanted it to be my last day, but not as a human, just as a drug addict. As I cut the skin, I started to bleed, and I could see the drops of blood hitting the floor, and then it was like time slowed down. I watched the drops roll off my wrist and slowly hit the floor in slow motion, and as I felt life starting to leave me, I felt my heart, not the pumping of the heart, but something inside beginning to fill up. I then started crying out that I did not want to end my life but wanted to live, as I ran to the house.

Talk about an emotional roller coaster ride. Wow!

When I went inside, I found my niece Kimmy and yelled, "Help me!" When she saw the blood all over me, she ran to pick up the phone to call my brothers and sisters, and without any delay, they all came, as well as the police.

You see, I believe God supernaturally removed the bullets from this earth because when I got clean, I tore that shed apart, and even when I moved from the property as I emptied the shed, I did not find one bullet, and even when my brother went for the gun, he could not find them. And that filling up, I felt in my heart was

God's love, which woke me up. I believe that when I go home to be with the Lord, He will open His hand and say, Remember these? Praise God for His loving power!

I call the part you just read "The Shed Experience."

*To some of you, it may be unbelievable, yet some may have experienced something similar. Either way, it happened, and it is as accurate as you taking your next breath, and until this day, I cannot explain it.

I hope I was able to paint a picture for you of how lame my childhood was and how deep the addiction was ruling my life. I would love to share more about how I lived in this addictive behavior, but that is not what this book is about. I only wanted to share a few key topics so you can understand where I was and how I got there.

Let's go to the next chapter, the beginning of an essential part of the book.

Chapter 6

Detox Time!

When my brothers and sisters were called, they called the police, thinking I would need the ambulance. I did not realize that trying to take your own life is against the law, and you can get jail time for it. Since the town I lived in was small enough for us to know almost all of the police officers, they did not take me to jail. Instead, they said to take me to the hospital for treatment.

I remember taking the drive, about thirty minutes away, but it felt like days. The wait was even longer. After a doctor looked at me and some other evaluations were done, they recommended that I go to a detoxification hospital for treatment. I do not know if you have ever been in this predicament, but I did not care for their recommendation. I will be fine; just let me sleep it off, and tomorrow will be better. After all, I cannot even kill myself, right? So what harm am I going to do to myself? That statement was not working too well, so we went home.

The next day, my brother made some phone calls, and one hospital told him they had a room, but they could only take me if I agreed to go. At the age of thirty-two, I did not want to go to jail or any hospital for treatment. I was in denial that I had a drug or drinking problem, and did not think I had any emotional issues for psychiatric therapy either. I was tired of the pain and wanted it to stop, so I attempted to take my life. You can see it as more of a cry for help than a nut case trying to kill himself—at least, that is what I thought. So after taking some time to think, I agreed to give it a chance. Well, it cannot be worse than my family having me under twenty-four-hour surveillance.

So in the fall of 1989, I was ready to embark on an adventure I had no idea what to expect. Am I going to be rejected, as everyone else has done? Are they going to be able to help? I wonder if they will drill my head with all that mental stuff. These were some questions I asked myself as my brother drove me to the hospital.

The first few days were the worst, not because I was coming off the drugs. But because of the drugs they had me on to come off the drugs I was on, they made me sick. But before long, I was drug-free and could join the rest of the patients on the wing. It was not that bad. For the first time in a long time, I was seeing things with a clear mind, as clearly as could be expected, coming off years of abuse.

We had to go to group meetings, and this is where I was introduced to AA (Alcoholics Anonymous) and NA (Narcotics Anonymous). These twelve-step programs are a fellowship for people seeking recovery from addictions. They both have books that recovering addicts will buy to help them understand the programs. Even though I did not have to buy one at that time, I still had to read them, and one day as we were reading, there was a part that used the saying,

"The God of our own understanding.[11]"

At that point, I jumped up and ran out of the room as one of the counselors ran after me.

He took me into the office and asked why I had run out. I told him that I wanted nothing to do with anything that was about God. The counselor had said that since I could not leave the program at this point for the next few days, how about if every time I came across the word "God," I would replace it with "good orderly direction," so I did not have to focus on God. I agreed. So for the rest of the time there, that is what I did, and it made it a lot easier to hear what was going on.

I spent a total of seven days there. I am so glad I am a fast learner and only had to do this once because I sure did not want to go through the drug withdrawals again, with the shakes and the little things floating around the room that, by the way, were not there.

There is not too much more to write about the time I spent in this hospital because it was a short period, but for many people who have gone through it, it is the most prolonged period they have ever experienced. If you are one of them, you know just what I mean.

Suppose you are reading this book and are having a hard time with addictions. In that case, the best thing you can do for yourself and your family is to admit you have a problem, find a good detoxification center to clear your thoughts, and then hopefully, you will be able to see how messed up your life is. Do not give up hope; you, too, can write a book on how you found the truth and the truth that set you free.

Here are some meanings.

Definition of *Detoxify* Merriam-Webster.com[12] (de tok'sefi'), v. t. –fied, -fy-ing. To rid of poison or the effect of poison. –de-tox'i-fi-ca'tion. N.

1. a: to remove a harmful substance (as a poison or toxin) or the effect of such from
2. b: to render (a harmful substance) harmless
3. to free (as a drug user or an alcoholic) from an intoxicating or an addictive substance in the body or from dependence on or addiction to such a substance
4. neutralize-to make chemically neutral. intransitive verb: to become free of addiction to a drug or alcohol

Definition of *Suicide* from Merriam-Webster.com

1. a: the act or an instance of taking one's own life voluntarily and intentionally, especially by a person of years of discretion and of sound mind b: ruin of one's own interests <political suicide> c: apoptosis <cell suicide>
2. one that commits or attempts suicide

Chapter 7

Why Am I Here & Where Am I Going?

When I left detox, I had to go straight into rehab at Riverside House in Philadelphia, Pennsylvania, for a thirty-day program. My mom and dad drove me there. It was nice seeing my parents doing something like this for me. It meant the world to me. It was just over an hour ride, and we talked almost the whole way; a big difference from when I would make road trips with them or my dad in the truck.

When we pulled into the driveway, my heart was beating fast, not with excitement but nervousness. I was not sure how to act. As I looked around, I could see it was a massive house on the Delaware River, not much of a yard, and very dreary looking. All kinds of thoughts were going through my mind, and I started sweating from nervousness. I had no choice. I had to stay, so my dad parked the car, and we went in. The inside was as dreary as the outside, with small rooms, except the large dining room, and there was a phone booth under the L-shaped stairway leading to the upstairs, where the South half was for the girls, and the North half was for men.

Now that I was in the process of being checked in, my parents left. I have to say something here about my dad. We did not realize that it would be a little cold, so I did not bring a jacket. When my dad and mom got home, my dad got my coat and drove back to the rehab so I would have one. How awesome was that? The dad I hated went out of his way for more than two hours so that I could be comfortable! I will never forget such a great act of love.

After checking in, they showed me to my bedroom, where I had to share it with two guys. This was not easy at first because of what I went through with my neighbor, but after a few days, I felt at ease because they turned out to be great guys. All the other guys had to share the hall bathroom, but we had our own, which was pretty cool.

In chapter 5, I mentioned that my girlfriend had left me a few days before my suicide attempt. So I was thinking about her and wanted to talk to her. I finally got her to visit me. During our visit, she agreed that because I was getting help, she would be home when I got out. Now that I no longer had to fill my head with thinking about her, I was able to focus on why I was there.

I will not give all the details of the thirty days, but I will provide you with the highlights. At first, it was challenging to be in a place where I was told what to do and when to do it. It felt like jail, and I do mean everything. I would say that for the first couple of weeks, I would read the word God as "good orderly direction," as I mentioned in the last chapter. During these first few weeks, I started to see clearly because I did not have the drugs in my system, but I still did not understand why I was there. You might know what I mean if you have been in rehab.

We would have many meetings and read different twelve-step program books, and as the days went by, I started to see why I was there. I was an addict, and to enjoy life, I had to get high, but there was a better way to live, according to those books. I was learning how to make my bed, clean my clothes, brush my teeth, and wash daily—the same things my mom told me!

They were trying to get me to accept myself as a person who was worth saving, and that is when I started to read the Serenity Prayer:

> *God grant me the serenity to accept those things I cannot change, the courage to change those things I can, and the wisdom to know the difference.*[13]

Those things I cannot change are the people around me: time, the weather, etcetera, and those things I can: is "me"—the way I think, treat people, or better yet, the way I act toward them; how I see myself, etcetera.

I held onto that prayer for the rest of the time I was there, and when I got out, I went and purchased a medallion and wore it around my neck. I did this for years because it helped me learn to put my trust in God.

There was one more thing that helped me there. Sitting at a table in the break room, I turned my head to a poem on the wall. As I read it, I noticed a clarity in what I was reading and a funny feeling in my stomach, like I felt that night in the shed. With the tears rolling down my face, I started to see a time in my life when I decided to walk away from someone.

That someone was God. I mentioned in earlier chapters about my past with the religion my mom had introduced to us, and I did not like what was being taught to me because they were making God out to be a mean person, so I wanted nothing to do with Him.

For years, I thought I had walked away from Him because He wanted nothing to do with me. Well, this poem says differently. The title of this poem is "Footprints in the Sand." You might know this poem; if you have never read it, Google it.

The part of the poem that hit home for me that day was: "It was then my brother when I carried you." When I first glanced at the picture, I saw the footprints, but I thought they were mine, and as I read down the poem, I heard those words, and I knew that God was speaking to me, telling me He never left me, and He never will. No matter what I have done or how I talked about Him, He loved me just the way I was and will be there to help me change. He will do the same for you.

> *Be strong and of good courage, do not fear nor be afraid of them, for the Lord your God, He is the One who goes with you. He will not leave you nor forsake you.* (Deuteronomy 31:6)

If you do not know God this way, read the poem to see if you hear Him... *Did you listen to Him this time?*

From then on, I was excited to see what He would do in my life. I started to find hope, courage, and excitement to finish the program and do whatever I needed to stay clean. From that time on, when I read the word "God," it no longer meant "good orderly direction." It meant "God," the big man, my Heavenly Father, the creator of heaven and earth, the one who loves me. Did you hear that? The one who loves me is a powerful word when it means something. For the first time, I felt like someone cared for me, about me, not looking to get something from me but to give me something—love! Wow, what an incredible feeling!

I was starting to deal with emotions and how to work problems out instead of reacting to them. I was learning to forgive not just myself but also others, even if I thought they were the ones who did wrong to me. One was my third-grade teacher, who gave me a failing grade. No, she did not give it to me; I am the one who earned it by not doing my work. I got mad because she would not let me make up the grade, so I could pass. This is how I was starting to change; learning to take responsibility for my wrongs and not blaming others.

I used to wear glasses, and one Saturday, during our Funtime playing volleyball, they broke. So I went to the counselor to see if there was any way I could get them fixed. She said I had to wait until Monday. Talk about learning patience. I could not see that far in front of me, and reading gave me a headache. That night, I tried to get aspirin, which they could not give me without a doctor's note, and told me to find one of the pressure points in my hand that would help me. By the way, it is between the thumb and forefinger.

What did I say in an earlier paragraph, learning to work out my problems instead of reacting? That one was not that easy, I tell you, but I made it through to Monday, and they got fixed. Praise God! I passed the test.

The time was getting near when I had to go out into the world, and I was so afraid that I was not going to stay clean, and that is one of the reasons I bought the Serenity Prayer, so I could make it through the rough times, even if it were one minute at a time. I was glad I was getting ready to leave, but I did not want to leave behind the friends I had made. I tried to keep in touch with them, but it failed fast. I think some of them relapsed, and I could never find a few.

I am very thankful to the counselors and any workers who had to deal with me, and even some of the other inmates who gave me words of encouragement that helped me make it to the end of the program. I pray to God for everyone and that one day, if they do not already have it, they will have what I have right now—peace!

Thank you, Riverside House!

Chapter 8

Let's Do The Twelve-Step!

One of the first things the counselors told me to do when I got home was to find a twelve-step meeting and attend it. I looked in the brochure and found one not far from me, which was good because I lost my driving privileges and had to walk. At that point, I did not care if it were Alcoholics Anonymous or Narcotics Anonymous, so long as the people I was going to be with understood what I was going through and could help me.

Because I was coming out of rehab, I had to go to aftercare at a local rehab for ninety days. I started to enjoy attending these meetings because I met people who went through the same thing I did, and we could discuss our shortcomings. During the next few months, I started to meet other people who were so friendly and willing to help me; they would pick me up for a meeting or give me a ride after one of the local ones. These guys started calling me their friend and wanted to spend time with me because they cared about me, not looking for something from me. I was beginning to feel like I was part of something.

We would go all over the state and sometimes the surrounding states to meetings to see what was going on and meet new people. We would call these road trips expanding our horizons. I started participating in meetings as chairman, or business meetings as treasurer or secretary, and going to jails to speak to the inmates. One year, I even became the hospitality chair for our yearly convention. I spent the next five years, at least six days a week, attending meetings and being part of a home group. Everything was great; I was not using anything and had no desire to.

I went through all the steps:

1. We admitted that we were powerless over our addiction and that our lives had become unmanageable.
2. We came to believe that a Power greater than ourselves could restore us to sanity.
3. We decided to turn our will and our lives over to the care of God as we understood Him.
4. We made a searching and fearless moral inventory of ourselves.
5. We admitted to God, to ourselves, and to another human being the exact nature of our wrongs.
6. We were entirely ready to have God remove all these defects of character.
7. We humbly asked Him to remove our shortcomings.
8. We made a list of all persons we had harmed and became willing to make amends to them all.
9. We made direct amends to such people wherever possible, except when to do so would injure them or others.
10. We continued to take personal inventory, and when we were wrong promptly admitted it.

11. We sought through prayer and meditation to improve our conscious contact with God as we understood Him, praying only for knowledge of His will for us and the power to carry that out.
12. Having had a spiritual awakening as a result of these steps, we tried to carry this message to addicts and practice these principles in all our affairs.[14]

Then I started to fall away from meetings until I stopped going altogether. I did not get to this point; I just felt there had to be more to life than Alcoholics Anonymous and Narcotics Anonymous meetings and repeatedly saying the same things. "Hi, my name is Anthony, and I am a recovering addict."

Do not get me wrong; there is much good being done in these meetings; I felt deep inside myself that something was missing, and I was no longer getting it from them.

I am not here to bash the twelve-step programs, but to hopefully show a better way to the truth about who you are and that you can be an overcomer over addictions. The promises of God are real, and they work, so I want to show how these steps are taken from the Bible, mostly from the content in the meaning of the word of God, then how you can use the word to be delivered from your addictions, no matter what kind.

Step 1 says that staying clean has to come first. The Bible says in Matthew 6:33 to put God first, and all these things will be added. What things? The help that is needed, *all* the truths of the written word.

Admitting that you are powerless over your addiction and that your life has become unmanageable is a great place to start. But the problem is, no matter what you do to fill the area, it only works for a short period. That is why you must keep working on it and attending those meetings until the day you die.

That is where I was! You will see later how I overcame this area.

Step 2 is right on, but the power greater than ourselves is the one who made us. Who better to understand the creation than the creator?

Who understands the well-known operating system, Microsoft Windows, more than anyone else, or who is the one who spent countless hours designing this now worldwide system, Bill Gates, or the people who work in the factories?

Bill Gates, of course!

Those people in the factory learn to understand how it works, but Bill Gates is the mastermind behind Windows, and that is who God is to us, the mastermind of all things (Revelation 1:8). Knowing the end from the beginning, knowing the ins and outs of our lives.

Just look at our bodies in how complex they are and how our doctors or scientists are trying to understand them completely, but they cannot! Only the mastermind behind the plan does, and that is why there is no way we evolved from a monkey.

If you are seeking recovery, take this second step and make God your higher power, not the chair you are sitting in.

Step 3 is a good step; it is a decisive step. It is a necessary step, but short in one area; we call this salvation (see 1 Thessalonians 5:5–11).

These twelve-step programs are trying to help people from all walks of life. The problem with addiction is addiction; no matter what your background is or the religion you stand on, the god of this world (Satan) does not care what your beliefs are. He is just out to destroy you because God loves you, and he hates God.

There is only one power source that can remove this controlling substance!

Keep reading!

Steps 4 through 9 are a form of deliverance, and it works. You must eliminate the garbage in your life to make room for God's love for you. Doing these steps without help from God will not be as effective and can leave skeletons in your closet.

Do not do it with shame, guilt, or resentment; be honest about it, and as things are revealed, ask God for forgiveness, and ask him to help you forgive yourself.

Step 5 can be overwhelming, so be careful about whom you pick to talk to and ensure it will not be someone who will write a story in the local paper. I found out that only those walking in the spirit of God can be trustworthy, and even then, you have to know their walk. God can do great work in this area with you and him in prayer time. Prayer is going to the king's throne and letting your petitions be known. Not everything needs to be said to every person.

James 5:16 in the amplified Bible says, *"To confess to one another, therefore, your faults and pray for one another, that you may be healed and restored to a spiritual tone of mind and heart."*

If you back it up a couple of verses, it says, "To call in the church elders and they should pray over him, anointing him with oil in the Lord's name."

See, not just anyone!

Step 6 is a step where you need to be willing to change. Are you ready? Remember, when you remove any character defects, you must fill them up with something good, or it will return (see Matthew 12:43–45 and Colossians 3:9–10).

Step 7 is to take action on a new life step. Believe that the one who made you loves you, and he understands you and wants you to seek after righteousness. He is the one leading the cheering section. He wants you to ask him to clean you so he can fill you with good things.

This is the real reason for the cross! (see Matthew 7:7–12, James 1:5–6, and 1 John 5:14–15).

Step 8 is remarkably close to Habakkuk 2:2, "And the Lord answered me, and said, Write the vision, and make it plain upon tablets, that he may run that reads it."

It is known that if you write it down, you will then see it and understand what you are working with. Now, notice that the step says that you became <u>willing</u> to make amends to them all; it does not say to go right out and spill your guts.

God says to make your petition known—him first, and then he will direct our paths to those willing to accept your apology.

This can be a straightforward step if you let it. Do not fret if you cannot do it before your thirty days. This is a lifetime effort. You do not get here in one day, so you are not going to get free from forgiveness in thirty days.

First, if you ask God into your heart, he is just to forgive you...some of your wrongs...*no...all* of your wrongs. He is the only person you need to worry about forgiving you...besides yourself (see Acts 26:18).

And this leads us into *step 9*: let God show you by his Holy Spirit. If you go to someone too early, it can be worse than the wrong you did in the first place. If the person is deceased, write a letter, and go to the grave to bury it or even burn it if you are concerned that someone might see it (see Leviticus 6:4–5).

Step 10 is a form of Luke 9:23–24, daily living in Him and not the drug, when I say the drug, I mean any mind-mood-altering substance!

Step 11 is to be applied to how much you want to leave your old life behind and trust in God for all he has for you without drugs (see Proverbs 3:5–6). Begin having a personal relationship with him and fellowship with other believers (see Ephesians 6:10–18).

That is the importance of the Lord's Prayer in Matthew 6: 9–13. Work on a relationship with him, not working to stay clean. He is faithful and just; all you need to do is ask. He said you have not because you ask not (see Matthew 7:8).

Step 12 is a church (see Acts 14:27, 16:5, 3 John 1:6). As you can see, God is through the twelve-step programs. I did not even touch on the twelve traditions of these programs. Many more scriptures can be used as a comparison, but I do not have room for them. If you read the word of God yourself, you will find them; just ask. He will guide you to them.

What I hope for from the writing of this book is that if you feel you are struggling with getting clean and maybe you have thirty, sixty, ninety, or even two, three, five years' worth of sobriety medals in your drawer and you want more, you need to read the next chapter. It will show you how I made it out of the KISS (Keep It Simple Stupid) mentality.

There is a saying you may have heard of. "Work smarter, not harder."

When applying it to your recovery, I would say, "That one day in His courts is better than one thousand days in a twelve-step program (Psalm 84:10)."

This is only part of how much God works in addiction, not just narcotics and alcohol, but all addictions. The name of Jesus is above *all names* (see Ephesians 1:21).

Chapter 9

Being Taken Out of the Miry Clay!

I want to tell you that going to those twelve-step program meetings worked for me, but I would have to do steps 4 through 9 again.

It did not!

God knew it was not going to work, and that is why he made a different way for me, and that is why this chapter is titled "Being Taken Out of the Miry Clay."

Miry Clay, what does this mean? We know it means muddy or a troublesome situation, but the word of God says it this way in Psalm 40:1–2:

"To the chief Musician, A Psalm of David: I waited patiently for the Lord, and He inclined unto me and heard my cry. He brought me up also out of a horrible pit, out of the MIRY clay, set my feet upon a rock, and established my goings."

There is much meaning in that scripture. I can write a sermon on the depth that is there. Simply put, he took me from death to life, from hell, the path I was on, to the light of the world, the rock—Jesus himself.

In the last chapter, I tried to show how the twelve-step programs were birthed from the word of God; they tried to come up with something that all addicts can relate to. I understand where they were coming from, but for the most part, if you want a drink of water from the well, you do not dig another hole on the side of what is already there. You grab the bucket tied on a rope, throw it down the hole, and when you pull it up, it will bring the bucket up, filled with water.

So is the way of the Christian walk—Jesus came to earth, was thrown down the pit, and was raised out of hell by the power of the Spirit of God so that we can drink of the truth and never thirst again. "Let anyone who is thirsty come. Let anyone who desires drink freely from the water of life." (Revelation 22:17, NLT)

As I said before, I was heavily involved with the twelve-step program after rehab for five years. I started to back off to once a week and maybe once a month. I stood away from people, places, and things until, one day, I met up with friends who used to go camping.

Okay, I can hear you saying, "Here it comes!"

Yes, here it comes—the truth on how a twelve-step program does not deliver you from the stronghold that addictions have on any one human being.

My ex-wife, Tammy, the same girl I spoke about in chapters 4 & 7, felt we could go out with them, and everything would be okay because it had been years since we drank or did any drugs. So we went out and purchased a camper and met up with them after work on Fridays. She was right…in the beginning! Until one day, I felt a bottle of white zinfandel would not hurt anything. I was not driving, and there were only a few of us; what harm would it do?

Should I keep going?

After one season, I was drinking not just at the campgrounds but at the house, wine and beer too. Then came the following season, round 2; I started to drink more, and now I was getting drunk all weekend. It was a colossal relapse that I thought would never occur. See, I used to think I was strong-willed and, with the time I had clean, I would never relapse.

That is how I felt!

Folks, this proves that the twelve-step dance ends when the music stops. The music keeps playing as long as you go to meetings, read their books, drink coffee, and smoke cigarettes.

"Can anyone else see it, or am I the only one?" *Bondage!*

Webster's Dictionary[15] calls this Slavery or involuntary servitude.

You might say, what makes that any different from going to church? My answer is that the church is in obedience to the word and building relationships with the saints as you learn how to hear God, not because it is the only way to stay clean. You can have a relationship with God and receive his power to overcome addictions without going to church.

I believe I was just as bad then as the day I stopped eight years prior—the way I acted, the way I spoke, the way I treated family and friends, and even the way I treated myself. Even though my life was spiraling downward, I thought it was still fine; at least I was not doing drugs or sticking needles in my arms. I was working during the week and drinking on the weekends…so what!

Does this sound like a sober man's words?

You might say, "Yeah, so what!"

I was not living the plan God had for me, one without drugs and addictions of all kinds...that is what!

Thank God we have a God of second chances!

My nephew used to come to my house, and we talked. Some would say he was preaching to me; I say he loved me. I understood some things he would say, from my mom, attending Catholic school, being an altar boy, and something I heard in the twelve-step meetings. Just the fact that he was family, and I loved him, I would let him talk out of respect. (I wish thousands of other people would think this way; it would make it easier to share God's love.)

Then one day, he said he was a born-again believer and that if I wanted to be set free, I too needed to accept Jesus as my Lord and Savior. I would tell him I have God. I do not need his Jesus. Yes, I was polite, not telling him to get the blank out of my house as someone did to me. Believe it! Someone said that to me. I will share this in the next chapter.

Remember in chapter 7, when I said I walked away from God, and then in rehab, I found Him? Well, nine years later, I was in a corner like a rat. I had a choice: I could lie down and do nothing but wait, run, or lash out and attack.

I thought everything was going great after all the dust settled with my second marriage. I thought my wife loved me, and many of our friends felt the same. I know drinking played a big part in my feelings, and here is the truth: I pushed her into watching porn, and our video/toy collection was growing.

I would say things to her that no husband should be speaking to his wife. The sad part about this is that I loved her and needed none of these things or actions in my life. I just thought it was fun and would add to our sex life.

> *Be careful on what you wish for; it just might come to pass!* (see Proverbs 18:21 and Ecclesiastes 5:6).

I could write a book on my marriages and the things I did wrong, showing how the drug mentality can destroy the best relationships in the world. But that is not what this book is about, so I will move on.

I was nasty, dirty, and ugly in every way. I was a father and a husband who was there in a physical sense but not in a spiritual one. And one day, a bomb was dropped on my lap; my ex-wife, Tammy, called me to tell me that she was not coming home anymore. She left me because she fell in love with our friend who went camping with us.

Are you ready for this?

This friend was of the same sex. Yes, you read it right! She was leaving me for another girl. She said she was gay and felt that way for a long time, as far back as a kid. Amazing how the devil will lie to someone and then amplify it.

I started to laugh and said, "Are you for real? You are saying you are in love with Chrissy?"

She said, "Yes, I can drive with my hand on her lap, and it feels good."

After we hung up, I started to cry at the shockwave that just hit me. I felt like I was drowning, and then it hit me; I knew who I had to turn to and what I needed to do. I picked up the phone and dialed my nephew's number, a number that I never remembered; I had to look it up any time I would call him because I did not call him that much.

But that day, October 5, 1998, I did not have to look it up. I believe God showed it to me because he knew what would happen, and he rejoiced. The phone rang until his voicemail picked up, so I left a message telling him I needed to talk to him.

Remember, I said we were camping every weekend? Well, that weekend was no different, minus two people—my wife and my friend's sister. I did not get to talk to my nephew until that weekend, three days after I left the message. I told him what had happened, and I felt God was calling me to receive Jesus—the same Jesus he had talked to me about all the past years. He said I should say the sinner's prayer to receive Him into my heart (read 1 John 1:9, 4:15, and Romans 10:9).

So, on October 9, 1998, I did just that.

God, forgive me!

Forgive me of all my sins!

I am sorry for not coming to you sooner!

Father, come into my heart and save me!

I believe that Jesus is your son, and you sent him here as a man for me because you love me!

I believe he died for all of my sins, past and future, was buried, and rose again!

I believe he descended to heaven and is seated at your right hand!

Thank you, Father. Amen!

Read John 3:16–18, 1 Corinthians 15:2–4, and Isaiah 53:5–12.

There is so much more I would love to share with you about my past, but I will tell you how my life turned around instead. That is why you are here. In chapter 3, I said I made a 180-degree turn from the direction God had planned for me; now, I made another 180-degree turn toward the original plan. Instead of being on the road of destruction, I am now on the road of life, eternal life. My body will die, but my spirit will live forever in heaven with God.

> *Enter through the narrow gate; for wide is the gate and spacious and broad is the way that leads away to destruction, and many are those who are entering through it. But the gate is narrow (contracted by pressure) and the way is straitened and compressed that leads away to life, and few are those who find it.*
> (Matthew 7:13–14, AMP)

I would like to tell you that my wife came back to me, but she did not. We divorced a couple of years later, and she left me with everything, including debt, so I had to go through bankruptcy. At the time of this writing, she was no longer with that girl and had remarried a wonderful guy. I praise God for leading her back to the truth that she was not gay. He does answer prayers.

Before moving on to the next chapter, this was the best time of my life, when my life was turned around—the best decision I ever made.

Chapter 10

I Can See Clearly Now!

In the last chapter, I told you how God removed me from the miry clay, a muddy pit. I believe God washed away all of my sins, forgave me of my wrongs, and stripped all those petty desires on that day. The only way I can explain it is through the title of this chapter.

It was like what took place with Saul (Paul) in Acts chapter 9:

Immediately, there fell from his eyes something like scales, and he received his sight at once; and he arose and was baptized.

I started to see the world in a new way—hatred turned into love, lying turned into truth, the flowers were brighter, the sky even looked awesome in the way the clouds would form into shapes, more than I could remember. For the first time in my life, I had a hunger to read the word of God.

I remember there was a day that all the steps of the twelve-step program came to mind, and I realized that Jesus was the higher power who put all of those steps into one ball and threw it down and said:

It is finished, Anthony! You are no longer an addict,

I have removed all desires and have delivered you. You no longer have to proclaim you are a recovering addict. I have washed you as clean as snow. That is why I died and shed my blood so you could be free. Rejoice, Anthony! You are a new man, a new creation in Christ. (2 Corinthians 5:17, Ephesians 4:24, Colossians 3:10)

How awesome is that!

This applies to you, too. Make sure to read the next chapter. It will change your life.

In the last chapter, I was truthful in telling you about me getting into porn and how our library of toys was growing. Well, one of those very first weekends when I went camping (Yes, I still kept camping with those friends!), I felt the Lord telling me to collect every one of those things I had because it was time to rid my house of that junk. I threw it all in a large bag and put it in the camper.

That night, after everyone went to bed, I took the bag out of the camper and placed it next to me by the fire. I threw it all, piece by piece, into the fire. I have to tell you, I have been around fires for many years, but that night that fire was special. As I threw each piece in, I felt more and more relieved over that strong addiction, not to mention that the fire was a bright orange color, like I had never seen before. After about two hours, I went to bed and slept peacefully. God does give rest to the weary!

I also mentioned in the last chapter about being told to get the blank out of a friend's house. Well, almost two months after accepting Jesus as my Lord and Savior, I was invited to a church where a man with a healing ministry was preaching. After three hours, I left the church to go home because I had to go to work the next day. As I was going down the road, I noticed I did not light up a cigarette.

Here is the best part, I did not feel like having one!

I was amazed at this point. I smoked two packs a day and tried to quit many times before, only having my ex-wife, Tammy, tell me to please get a pack of cigarettes because I was driving her crazy.

I did not know how to handle this since this born-again life I now had was all new to me. I knew that as I was sitting in that meeting, the guy asked if there was anyone who had an addiction problem that they would want to be set free from to stand. So I stood up for the drinking since it was only a few weeks since I stopped. I felt that if I could be clean for nine years and go back to drinking, I might get a prayer for a complete release. Now know this, I had no thought in my mind about smoking. I had decided the last time I tried to quit that it was hopeless for me to stop.

When I got home, I told the Lord before going to bed, "Lord, I do not know what just happened to me or why, but if this is not you, I will find out in the morning." The mornings were always the toughest whenever I tried to quit, but when I woke up the following day, guess what? I had no desire to have a cigarette. Wow!

Up to this point, I was experiencing some remarkable things, but nothing like this; it was the full power of God's love. I went to work and had to do a test later that day. God's word says in first John 4: 1, "Beloved, do not believe every spirit, but test the spirits, whether they are of God; because many false prophets have gone out into the world."

I had four cigarettes left in the pack, so I lit one and took a drag; it tasted nasty, and I mean *nasty*! I put it out and threw the box away and have not had a cigarette since, twenty-one years at the time of this writing, no desire, no withdrawal, not even weight gain—*nothing*!

Friend, if this does not make you think about how alive God is and how much He loves you, you'd better check your pulse; you might not be alive.

Getting back to the point I was making about my friend. When I went to his house one night, he asked me why I was not smoking. I testified on what the Lord had done, and he told me to get the f____ out of his house. I grabbed my coat, headed for the door, and never returned.

Do you want to know what God says about this?

"And whoever will not receive and accept and welcome you nor listen to your message, as you leave that house or town, shake the dust from your feet" (Matthew 10:14, AMP).

I saw him once after that, and I have prayed for him every day since that night. May God bless you, Larry, and I want you to know I love you, and so does God.

Do you want to know why he acted that way?

His mom had died a few years previously, and he blamed God for it.

Just a note: God is a giving God, not a taker. It is the things of this world (*sin*) that cause death, not God (see Romans 6:23). He has made a way (Jesus) for us, so we do not have to die a spiritual death—that is what being born-again is all about. He does not say we will live forever here on earth. After the fall of Adam and Eve, these bodies are born to die, but our spirit will live forever in heaven with him (see John 3:15).

Where is your spirit going to be?

Shortly after I began my Christian walk, I had to move into my camper so I could rent my apartment to my nephew to help pay the bills. After looking back, I think that had to be one of the essential times in my life because God showed himself to me in many different ways, without any doubt.

I was falling deeper and deeper in love with him, and he was revealing himself to me more and more each day. I was so on fire; I could not stop talking about this new love of my life. I am glad my ex-wife Tammy left me; it pushed me to Jesus, maybe years beforehand. No one knows the time nor the hour but God. I hope if you do not already know him or perhaps even live right for him, you will meet me in chapter 11.

Do you remember back in chapter 8, I tried to show you how God's word was the birthing of the twelve-step programs? And I mentioned steps 4 through 9? I know firsthand that God can take us through deliverance without another human being involved. Since I was by myself, I spent a lot of time alone. Well, not completely alone, I did have God. There were countless hours of throne room–type prayer where God would show me things from my past, and as he did, I would repent, and God would forgive, and I would repent, and God would forgive, and so on and so on.

By the time God was done with me, I was so free; I could feel it—peace was all over me. It is still that way today, which is why my hair is black at sixty-four. Some of my family think I dye it, and when I tell them I do not, they call me a liar. But it is just the peace of God in my life.

How would you like to read another testimony?

I had a GMC pickup, and one night I took my daughter to Egg Harbor City before going to my bowling league in Hammonton. It was raining, and on my way back to Hammonton, I felt this impression not to drive the outside lane, next to the shoulder, on the White Horse Pike; it was a four-lane highway with two lanes in each direction. When I got to the bowling alley, I pulled into the parking spot, and when I stopped, the right front of the truck dropped. When I got out, I saw the tire under the truck.

There was nothing I could do then, so I went into the bowling alley. (I said I was set free!) When I told my buddies what happened, they said my tie-rod broke, and I was blessed that I was not driving; it could have flipped the truck.

Can you see it? Can you see how God intervenes?

If you listen closely, you can hear him speak, too! When I was driving and felt the impression not to ride the outside lane, it was raining so heavily that all that water on the side of the road would have put pressure on the tie-rod and broken on the road, not in the bowling alley parking spot.

Wow, talk about God's love!

It does not stop there. I had no money except the few dollars I needed to bowl, and I was not even making ends meet at home. How was I going to get the truck fixed, or for that matter, towed? After the league was done, one of my friends gave me a ride home, and when I got there, I went straight to one of my prayer closets (a place where it is just you and God). The garage was the pick for that night, and I started to pray. I remember crying to God, saying something like, "God, I need your help. I have no money to fix my truck or get it towed home. I have been serving you faithfully and have helped people with their problems, and now it is time for me to receive." I just told you the short version; I prayed for at least an hour and then went to bed.

The next day was Sunday, and a friend picked me up to attend church. He asked me what I would do about my truck, and I told him I did not know; it was in God's hands. When we got to church, I was fellowshipping with some of the guys when a brother approached me and shook my hand. Inside that hand was a fifty-dollar bill; he said God told him to give it to me. I thought this *should be enough to tow the truck home. Praise God!*

Wait, it is not over!

A few minutes later, someone else walked up to me and said that last night when he was in prayer (about the same time I was in worship, by the way), God told him to give his car away, the one he was going to sell to help him with college tuition. I do not have to tell you how I felt; I think you might know, or maybe you do not.

Praise God!

Wait, it is not done!

The next day, when I went to work and was testifying about my weekend experience, one of the guys asked me what I would do about the truck. I said I was not sure; I had fifty dollars to tow it home, but did not have the money to fix it, or I could use the fifty dollars to put the car on the road, but then I would not be able to tow the truck home.

He turned to me and said, "I will give you $1,500 for the truck just as soon as you can bring me the title." I said, "What! You will buy my truck right now?"

He said, "Yes, I will go get it from the bowling alley, so you do not need to get it towed."

Holy smokes! What a new day can do when you are in the kingdom of heaven. I not only had a running car, but I also had the money to put it on the road and pay for some of my bills.

I will repeat it. *Praise God!*

The guy who gave me his car went to college without needing the money he would have received from selling the vehicle. God took care of that man. Here is the scripture for you: see Luke 6:38.

Do you want to know something? God had been on my side even before I said the sinner's prayer because five years earlier, I paid $5,000 for that truck, had made much money with it, and still ended up with $1,500.

God does care for his children, even if you do not want to believe what I am saying here.

"I love you, God. You are awesome in every way!" Maybe one day, God will direct me to write a book of testimonies or even the miracles I have seen; there have been many of them. I saw the healing power not only in my own life but right in front of my own eyes,

✝ hearing restored
✝ tumors dissolved
✝ blind eyes opened
✝ short leg made even with the other leg
✝ marriages restored, and
✝ children returned to their parents

One time at a weekly Bible study, a man came in drunk, could not even stand up, his eyes bloodshot and slurring his words. We prayed for him, asking God to deliver him from this addiction. About fifteen minutes into the prayer, his countenance changed; his eyes were no longer bloodshot, his speech was more precise, and he could stand on his own without falling. Praise God!

Okay, one more before we move to the next chapter, the most crucial chapter in the book, so do not stop now. You made it this far, my friend; keep going! One day, I was going to my pastor's house for a men's Bible study with His Hands Ministry. I was driving about 50 mph. About fifty yards from me, a car pulls out in front of me from a convenience store. I assume they never saw me coming because they were moving extremely slowly.

As I approached the car, I realized I was not going to slow down in time without hitting them, so I pulled to the shoulder of the road, applying the brakes. I lost control of the van in the dirt and was headed for a cluster of trees, not large trees, but I saw small trees do some damage just as well, so I yelled out the name of Jesus, and within seconds, I found myself looking over my left shoulder at the dirt.

When I realized what had just happened, I undid my seat belt and hit the button for the passenger's window to roll down so I could climb out. Some passing cars had stopped, and people ran to the van to find out if I was okay. I remember looking out the windshield at one guy peeking in with a wow look on his face; I think he was expecting me to be dead or at least unconscious.

I climbed up and got on top of the van; we can say it was the side of the van, at least it used to be, and jumped off. By this time, someone had called the police and said they were on their way. The car that caused all this never stopped; I think they did not even know what they did. Forgive them, Father!

As I walked around the van, I was amazed to see how minor the damage was, and my first thought was, *Let us flip this lousy boy over so I can make it to Bible study.* Then a lady walked up with an awed look and said, "I have never seen a vehicle flip over on its side with such grace. It was like it was in slow motion. Someone was with you, sir!"

When the police arrived, the officer's first thought was that I was speeding and lost control. When I told them a car pulled out in front of me, and I took the shoulder not to hit them, I do not think he believed me at first until the person living across the street came over and told the officer that a car pulled out in front of the van and was going slowly. Thank you, ma'am!

After I was picked up and returned home, we went to the salvage yard to look at the van, and I took some pictures; then, we went to the site to see what it looked like. I was amazed to see the tire marks in the dirt and how close they came to the tree, and then I remembered the front of the van, and how there was no damage to the front right bumper. So after a closer look, there was no way I could not have hit the tree.

At that point, I remembered what that lady had said to me and realized that God was with me, and my guardian angel must have taken that van and gracefully flipped it so I would not hit the tree head-on.

Please check the website for some photos of the accident. I made some notations on some pictures so you can get a better feel for what I mean. You will see how the damage on the driver's side is not that bad, and one would think that if a car is going 50 mph, loses control, and hits a tree (that is, if they hit the tree), and because of the force, would flip over, it would slide. This is not how it happened; it was converted over and laid down on the side with minimal damage, and in the one picture, you can see that the grass is not torn up.

Yes, it did get totaled by the insurance company because they said it would cost more to repair it than it was worth. But to me, my wife lost her van, but I got to see God's working power in my life again.

Can I say it once more?
Praise God!

I am sharing all these testimonies with you in the hope that you will see how God showed himself to me, which is why I put them in this chapter. It made me see clearer every day on how real he is real, and yes, he is alive and well.

Before I move you to the next chapter, I would like to explain how my life is now.

I am not a man who likes to boast or be put on a pedestal, but I need to share with you where I am today so you can see how opposite I am from the beginning of the book and how different my life has become.

You may have noticed that at the end of the last testimony, I mentioned that the van in the accident was my wife's. That is because God blessed me with my third wife, Laura, of almost twenty years at the time of this revised writing.

Unfortunately, in the late fall of 2018, I received a letter from my oldest sister that would expose some things that I had done as a young kid and led to those earlier years of addiction. Laura had asked me to go to counseling, but after researching the situation, I decided not to go through with it. I felt no need to since it had been over forty years, and I am no longer that person. In the following months, it caused a strain on our marriage, leading Laura to leave, and in July 2020, sadly, our divorce was finalized.

I still praise God for her and the time we had together. Even though marriage number three ended, I still pursue what God has for me and will not allow the past to dictate my future.

I did get to speak to one counselor a little bit, and a pastor about it, and the conclusion was that all parties affected by it, and God, have forgiven me, so I just needed to work on forgiving myself. So I had to use my books on forgiveness to help me work through this. On one of the affirmations, "Dead and Alive," one of the confessions is, "I am no longer in resentment; I am now in forgiveness." So, in other words, I had to go through deliverance to get where I am today. Even though I am not proud of this, I found more of God's grace and the meaning of true forgiveness. At the time of the original writings for the book, I had no recall of this action. In this book revision, I made some changes to the text.

You will most likely understand how blackouts work if you are a drinker or into heavy drugs. If not, please know that the mind, or brain, sometimes will bury thoughts and even emotions so deeply that a person has a difficult time recalling those thoughts or actions. Many books explain blackouts and how they work. Dr. Caroline Leaf wrote one of the best books I read about the brain. Please consider reading up on this subject to learn more about how our brains work and how complicated, at the same time incredible, this three-pound organ is. I like how the animated movie "Inside Out" identifies the depth of human emotions and how one can bury those emotions or thoughts. It gives a visual of how the brain can work. I have watched it twice and do not even have any little kids around.

During the time of writing my first book, I tried to recall things that happened to me that drove me to the lifestyle I had for over sixteen years. That is one of the reasons it took me almost three years to complete the manuscript, as I mentioned in previous chapters about the earlier years of my youth and how I felt about not having anyone in my life to guide me. I missed something I never imagined would be part of my life. I felt not to expand on each life story since the original thought behind writing the book was to help people with addictions and not to make it a complete autobiography.

As time rolled on from the release date, I learned that I needed to make a few corrections. Like, the actual time my daughter was born that was mentioned in Chapter Four, or my sister pointing out to me that one of the pics I have in the back of the book I thought was a picture of all my siblings, when in fact, one of the girls is my neighbor. Which were corrected when my publisher closed their doors, and I had to do self-publishing and was able to make those corrections. And now that brings me back to my blessings that keep coming no matter what happens in my life.

God had also blessed me with the adoption of Laura's grandson as my son, who lived with us when he was six months old. Today, he is twenty and in the Air Force.

I no longer feel like I did in chapter 1 with all those destructive emotions. I am confident, trustworthy, dependable, and dedicated to God and the church. I know I am loved and no longer feel lonely. I know that God is in control of my life, so life is not disappointing anymore, and I am not ashamed to be an Ordille. Today, I have a brother who is there for me, allows me to be with him, and makes me feel welcome 24-7; his name is Jesus. I hold an associate degree in Christian studies and a bachelor's degree in church ministry, and I received an ordained minister license through The Sure Foundation Theological Bible Institute. I was asked to be a Deacon at my local church a few years ago.

Does that sound like the same person who lived the first chapters and is now the author of three books?

Today, I still have dreams, visions, and goals, but now they are from the Lord and have a whole new meaning. I can go on and on, but I need to say, "Folks, if God can do this for me, he will do it for you if you let him."

Now we come to the time you need to decide; this will be the most crucial decision ever. I will see you in the next chapter.

This part was added to this book before going to the publishers during the first edition.

In chapter 4, I talked about my son, some of our relationships, and how God has to do good work on this mess. Right before the first edition's final touches, I had confirmation from God to take a trip with my family to see him. My son mentioned a couple of months earlier that he wanted us to come up. I was afraid to go because I did not know how it would turn out; that was my flesh speaking, not what my spirit wanted to do. Just as we set the time to go, I got word from my job that the project we were waiting for got the go-ahead to start, and that I would have to be there. I mentioned this to my son, and he told me he was disappointed that I would not be able to come up; he wanted to see me. I told him I had to wait for a pre-construction meeting to find out the details to determine if I could make it.

This was only a few days before the weekend that we set aside to go. That weekend was special because it was my grandson's birthday, and what better time to go? At that meeting, I learned that it would not start until close to Christmas, so I was free to take a vacation. As I sat there thinking about how hard it would be for me to take the road trip and how afraid I was to see my son, I asked God one question: "God, what am I supposed to do?"

He answered me with, "You need to go!"

This trip was about eight hours away and would not be pleasant because when I relocated to Texas, I drove 1,700 miles in thirty-two hours and did something to my right leg where I could not go more than two to three hours at a time. We made plans to drive halfway with a hotel overnight stay.

I made it to the house without a problem, had a beautiful weekend with my son and grandson, and went to their church on Sunday morning.

Yes, I said their church! He was attending church with a remarkable man of God as his preacher. Praise God for his faithfulness! And I was able to drive home with very minimal pain.

Here is a text I received from him a couple of weeks later, replying to one of mine:

> 'Love you too. And just to let you know, you most definitely have the Lord walking with you. Since you have been here, I have felt different. A happier difference, more upbeat about the future, I feel very strong lately.'

God is great all the time!

One last testimony before moving on...

After I left Remington College, a job that God opened the door to when I relocated to Fort Worth, Texas, in 2007, for ten years, I was healed in my legs from being unable to drive long distances. I started to drive for Lyft, and in the first year, I could go over 65,000 miles and 80,000 in the second year.

Praise God!

Chapter 11

Come and Go with Me!

I hope this book has blessed you, and if you are struggling with an addiction of any kind or sickness in your body, know that God wants to heal you and set you free. In Luke 4:18, after the account when Jesus was being tempted by the devil (see chapter 4:1), he was teaching in the synagogue and was given the book of the prophet Isaiah when he read:

> *The Spirit of the Lord God is upon me, because the Lord has anointed and qualified me to preach the Gospel of good tidings to the meek, the poor, and afflicted; He has sent me to bind up and heal the brokenhearted, to proclaim liberty to the [physical and spiritual] captives and the opening of the prison and of the eyes to those who are bound, To proclaim the acceptable year of the Lord [the year of His favor] and the day of vengeance of our God, to comfort all who mourn* (Isaiah 61:1-2 AMP).

Also, for healing, you can read Isaiah 53:4–5, 58:8, Jeremiah 33:6, Matthew 4:23, 9:35, Luke 9:11, and Acts

10:38 (only a few of the many places in the Word that state that healing is for today).

At the time of the revised copy of this book in 2021, I was seven years caffeine-free; I went on a twenty-eight-day fast for our nation and had no desire to go back to drinking coffee when it was over. So God's power works in every addiction we are struggling with, my friend.

> *The apostle Peter says it this way; So brace up your minds; be sober (circumspect, morally alert); set your hope wholly and unchangeably on the grace (divine favor) that is coming to you when Jesus Christ (the Messiah) is revealed*
>
> (1 Peter 1:13 AMP).

The title of this chapter is "Come and Go with Me." You might be saying, "Go where with you? Why do you want me to join you? Why must one be born again? What does baptism mean, and how or when should I?" Of course, I am talking about going to heaven, and

I want you to go with me because God loves you and does not want to see you go to hell, and neither do I. The scriptures say that Jesus said these words to Nicodemus, a ruler among the Jews:

> *Jesus answered him, I assure you, most solemnly I tell you, that unless a person is born again (anew, from above), he cannot ever see (know, be acquainted with, and experience) the kingdom of God. Nicodemus said to Him, How can a man be*

born when he is old? Can he enter his mother's womb again and be born?

Jesus answered, I assure you, most solemnly I tell you, unless a man is born of water and [even] the Spirit, he cannot (ever) enter the kingdom of God. What is born of [from] the flesh is flesh [of the physical is physical]; and what is born of the Spirit is spirit. Marvel not [do not be surprised, astonished] at my telling you, you must all be born anew (from above).

(John 3:3–7 AMP)

He who believes and is baptized will be saved; but he who does not believe will be condemned.

(Mark 16:16)

Being baptized is not when you are a baby. One must be aware of this decision to fulfill the truth of the scriptures. I have searched the scriptures and found nothing that tells us to baptize our babies. I have seen where it tells us to dedicate them, 1 Samuel 1:11, 26–28 (Jehovah is Jesus). A baby dedication is a ceremony in which parents make a commitment that they will train that child up in the ways of the Lord (Proverbs 22:6). So, to answer this question, one should be baptized after receiving the gift of salvation and not before. Any spiritual leader can baptize you, and it can even be done in your bathtub or swimming pool.

Before I lead you in the salvation prayer, I would like to share a short teaching on salvation and what it means so you know what and why you are asking God into your heart. In the Webster's Dictionary[16], the meaning is:

1. the act of saving from harm or loss.
2. the state of being thus saved.
3. a means of being thus saved.
4. deliverance from the power and penalty of sin.

The most famous scripture in the world is John 3:16:

> *For God so greatly loved and dearly prized the world He gave up His only begotten Son, so that whoever believes in (trust in, clings to, relies on) Him shall not perish (come to destruction, be lost) but have eternal (everlasting) life.* (AMP)

So because God gave Jesus, it must be a gift to all who believe in him. It is God's grace on humanity because sin's wages are death.

In Revelation, the last book of the Bible, which is the account of Apostle John being caught up to heaven through a vision, and in one of his encounters, where he was face-to-face with an angel (a messenger of God) who told him not to put a seal on the book of prophecies, which is the whole Bible, not just revelations. The reason is that at the return of Jesus, he will bring his wages and rewards to repay and render to each one just what his actions and work merit. You can read about this in Revelation 22, starting in verse 10 to verse 16. And in verse 17, it reads like this:

> *And the Holy Spirit and the bride say Come! And let him who is listening say, Come! And let*

> *everyone come who is thirsty who is painfully conscious of his need of those things by which the soul is refreshed, supported, and strengthened; and whoever earnestly desires to do it, let him come, take, appropriate, and drink the water of life without cost.* (also see Isaiah 55:1) The word bride here means the church, and the true Christians.

Are you listening? Is your soul crying out because it is thirsty? You do not know how to quench that thirst. That is why you rely on addictions, hoping they will go away. But it does not; the only water that can do it is the water of life, Jesus himself. What are your wages and rewards going to be? The wages found in Romans 6:23, and will the rewards be the first half of verse 11 of Revelation, or will they be the second half of that verse?

> *For the wages of sin is death, but the free gift of God is eternal life through Christ Jesus our Lord.*
> (Romans 6:23)

Grace: kindness, favor.

> *But God, who is rich in mercy! Because of His great love which He loved us, even when we were dead in sins (trespasses), has quickened (made) us together (alive) with Christ, (by GRACE you are saved;) and have raised us up together, and made us sit together in heavenly places in Christ Jesus: that in the ages to come He might show the exceeding riches of His grace in His kindness toward us through Christ Jesus. For by grace you*

> *are saved through faith; and that not of yourselves: it is the gift of God: not of works, lest any man should boast.*
>
> (Ephesians 2:4–9)

Regarding the location of the sinner's prayer in the Bible? Well, there is not one mentioned; it is only implied. The basis of the sinner's prayer comes from Romans 10:9–10.

> *That if thou shalt confess with thy mouth the Lord Jesus, and shalt believe in thine heart that God hath raised him from the dead, thou shalt be saved. For with the heart man believeth unto righteousness; and with the mouth confession is made unto salvation.*

Please note that the salvation prayer below is not official but a sample prayer to follow when asking Jesus into your heart. You can pray to God in your own words. Are you ready? Are you prepared to lay your life down for the work of the cross? I hope you said yes because it is time for you to join me at the lamb's dinner table prepared for you.

Read this prayer out loud if you must stop and find a place. Do it, please; you will not regret it. Take your time and listen to the words. Let them sink into your spirit.

Dear God in heaven, I come to you in the name of Jesus. I acknowledge to you and myself that I am a sinner, and I am sorry for my sins and the life that I have lived; I need your forgiveness. Father, I know I cannot get rid of this addiction alone; that only you, and you alone, can take it from me and deliver me. Make me clean as snow as you did with Anthony; give me the same power he has seen so I can also see clearly. I believe that your only begotten son, Jesus Christ, shed his precious blood on the cross at Calvary and died for my sins, and I am now willing to turn from my sin. You said in Romans 10:9 that if we confess to the Lord our God and believe in our hearts that God raised Jesus from the dead, we shall be saved.

Right now, I confess Jesus as the Lord of my soul. With my heart, I believe that God raised Jesus from the dead. At this very moment, I accept Jesus Christ as my personal savior, and according to your word, right now, I am saved. I thank you, Jesus, for your unlimited grace. I thank you, Jesus, that your grace always leads to repentance. Therefore, Lord Jesus, transform my life so I may bring glory and honor to you alone and not myself. I thank you, Jesus, for giving me eternal life. Amen!

If you just said this prayer and meant it with all your heart, I believe you just got saved and are born again. All of heaven is rejoicing, so rejoice, my friend, because you will be sitting with me at the lambs' dinner table when he returns for us. Please let me know by visiting my website, and I would love to add you to a list of names I will be praying over.

You may ask, "Now that I am saved, what's next?" First, you must get into a Bible-based church and study God's Word. Once you have found a church home, you will want to become water baptized. By accepting Christ, you are baptized in the Spirit, but it is through water baptism that you show your obedience to the Lord. Water baptism is a symbol of your salvation from the dead. You were dead, but now you live, for the Lord Jesus Christ has redeemed you for a price! The price was his death on the cross.

If you are born once, you will die twice, but whoever is born twice will die once!

One of the first things you need to start with is forgiveness! You start with forgiving yourself and then anyone who has hurt you. This frees you up for the Holy Spirit to fill you with the love of God.

If you would like to use a workbook to help you with forgiveness, look for "Overcome Addiction by God's Grace: 12-Steps to Freedom Workbook." It is part of a 12-step program I developed in 2016. Just visit my website.

I hope you enjoyed this book and that it was a help in finding yourself. Remember, addiction is a stronghold; only through the help of Jesus Christ can you overcome it and put it under your feet. Stay in the Word, grow in the Spirit, and know you are loved.

The next chapter is a section filled with affirmations to help you know who you are in Christ; these are here for you to read any time you need them.

Chapter 12

Affirmations

*Affirmat*ions from Webster's New World Dictionary:[17]

1. The act of affirming
2. Something affirmed; positive declarations; assertion

These help you think positive thoughts in your life and declare that you are in Christ Jesus. Since this book was about addictions, I felt to include them to help you.

Are you tempted?

<u>HERE IS HOW YOU CAN OVERCOME TEMPTATION</u>.

You need to know who you are. You are a child of God. You are the righteousness of God. The devil questioned Jesus's identity, so we are no different. What did Jesus do? He quoted Deuteronomy. He is not making up scripture. Whatever he would have said would become scripture, but he held fast to the Word. Go back to the simple truths of the Word. Romans 12:1–2 says, "And be not conformed to this world: but be transformed by the renewing of your mind." Bring your mind to the subjection of the Word by feeding your mind the Word of God. If you are dealing with smoking and drinking, your body is the temple of the Holy Spirit. Get in that Word, renew your mind, and replace those thoughts with more excellent ones. Open your mouth. Confess any scripture you know that will consume the thoughts that have consumed you. God has given you this Word so you can be free.

Do not fall into temptation. Read 1 Corinthians 10:13. The devil wants you to think, "I do not know if I can handle this temptation." But this verse says that God will not allow you to be tempted beyond what you can handle. So if you find yourself in a situation, be encouraged. You can get out of it. It is not impossible.

HERE'S HOW TEMPTATION WORKS:

Fantasy and flirtation fall first because you allow them to grow in your mind. Then you begin to flirt with it. Then you fall.

We must deal with it in the early stages of fantasy and thought life. That way, if we stumble, we can still pull back. You cannot look at pornography. You have to watch over your heart with all diligence. You must be careful where you go, whom you hang around with, and what you watch because you are responsible for watching over your heart.

2 Peter 2:9 says, "Then the Lord knows how to deliver the godly out of temptations and to reserve the unjust under punishment for the Day of Judgment." He gives us the knowledge of how to avoid it ourselves. There is only one way not to be tempted—Your flesh

will provide you with impulses, so do not adhere to it. Repeat, I take up my cross, and I die to this.

2 Timothy 2:22 says, "Flee also youthful lusts; but pursue righteousness, faith, love, peace with those who call on the Lord out of a pure heart." Run with all your might. Run as if your life depended on it. Run with them that call on the Lord from a pure heart.

HERE ARE A FEW SIMPLE STEPS TO HELP YOU:

If you are born again, you are a new creature. God says, "Be ye holy, even as I am holy." He says this over you. He says you already are holy. He made you in his image. If you have made Jesus your Lord, then as he is, so are you in this world. The same Spirit that raised Jesus from the dead lives inside you.

Repent of your sins; to repent is to change how you think. When you try to take a shortcut to change outward, you will never be able to change. Romans 12:1–2 says:

> *I beseech you therefore, brethren, by the mercies of God, that you present your bodies a living sacrifice, holy, acceptable to God, which is your reasonable service. And do not be conformed to this world, but be transformed by the renewing of your mind, that you may prove what is that good and acceptable and perfect will of God.*

It is your thought life. As I got my mind renewed, my desires changed. You are not going to be able to strong-will yourself into doing it. Addictions can be delivered instantly, but sometimes it is just that you need your mind renewed. It is like a pig; you can dress him up and make him look good, but when he sees mud, he is going to jump in. Why? Because he has not changed on the inside.

Know that the curse is broken.

Addictions are sometimes passed down from generation to generation. The Bible says that God will visit the iniquity of the fathers up into the third and fourth generations. But you can decide to be one of the four curses or the first generation of blessings. It would be best if you made that decision today.

HOW DO YOU BREAK THE CYCLE OF THE CURSE OF ADDICTION?

1. You have got to sow the opposite of what your parents reaped. If they reaped negative things in their lives, you have to sow the opposite into someone else's life.
2. You have got to identify with the new bloodline. I am not a part of the generation of my parents any longer. I am a part of the new bloodline. Jesus became a curse for me. Galatians 3:13 says, "Christ has redeemed us from the curse of the law, having become a curse for us, for it is written, 'Cursed is everyone who hangs on a tree.'" The generational curses died on the cross with Him when He died on the cross.

3. Do not retaliate. Do not react to what people have done to you. Do not try to get back at somebody, your relatives, parents, kids, or whomever.
4. Accept personal responsibility. You are responsible for saying to whatever thing needs to be gone, "Be gone." You are responsible for speaking to the mountain of curses, "Be thou removed! And cast into the sea."
5. You have got to make different choices than your parents made. If you do not, that stuff will follow you to your grave. You need to be set free. Now, it is not a feeling. Breaking free from a curse is not a feeling. It is a decision. It appropriates the blood of Jesus.

Decide to be the first generation of blessings. Decide that from this day forward, you choose life, and you identify with the bloodline of Jesus. Identify what He says. He said, "It is written," and you say, "It is written." He says, "You are holy," and you say, "I am holy." He says, "You're more than a conqueror," and you say, "I'm more than a conqueror."

You are already made free by the blood of Jesus, and he became that curse for you.

Hallelujah!

There are more than three hundred scriptures about fear, so here are some confessions of faith you can speak over your life. Use them every day if you have to, but use them.

† I can do all things through Christ who strengthens me (Philippians 4:13).

- ✝ I am not afraid because God is my salvation and I trust Him (Isaiah 12:2).

- ✝ I am not tormented because all fear is cast out in God's perfect love (1 John 4:18).

- ✝ I do not fear nor am I dismayed, because God is with me. God makes me strong and helps me and upholds me with His victorious and righteous right hand (Isaiah 41:10).

- ✝ I do not fear, for God has redeemed me and called me by name—I am His (Isaiah 43:1).

- ✝ The Lord is my helper, and I will not fear what man can do to me (Hebrews 13:6).

- ✝ I avoid snares because I do not fear man, but I place my trust in the Lord and therefore I am safe (Proverbs 29:25).

- ✝ I am strong and courageous, delivered from fear, because the Lord my God goes with me. He will not fail me nor forsake me (Deuteronomy 31:6).

- ✝ I have not received the spirit of bondage again to fear, but I have received the spirit of adoption whereby I cry "Abba, Father" (Romans 8:15).

- ✝ I listen to the Lord, therefore, I dwell safely and I am quieted from the fear of evil (Proverbs 1:33).

† I will not fear nor be discouraged, for the Lord my God has set the land before me—I will go up and possess it (Deuteronomy 1:21).

† I will not fear, for the Lord my God shall fight for me (Deuteronomy 3:22).

† I do not fear, for it is my Father's good pleasure to give me the kingdom (Luke 12:32).

† I am not afraid of bad news, for my heart is fixed, trusting in the Lord (Psalm 112:7).

† I am strong and courageous, not fearful and dismayed for the Lord is my strength, my song and my salvation (Isaiah 12:2).

† I walk in the peace that Jesus has left for me, not peace as the world gives. My heart is not troubled neither is it afraid (John 14:27).

† I am a new creation—a new person altogether in Christ Jesus. Old things have passed away; all things have become fresh and new (2 Corinthians 5:17).

† I have been made the righteousness of God. I am completely justified by faith apart from the works of the law. Therefore, I have peace with God today and I can stand in His presence without guilt, shame or a sense of inferiority (Romans 5:1-2, Corinthians 5:21).

✝ Jesus has reconciled me by His death and presents me to the Father unblameable, unaccusable and without reproach, since I continue in faith firmly established and steadfast, not moved away from the truth of God's Word that I have heard (Colossians 1:22–23).

✝ The Father has qualified me to share in this inheritance and has drawn me to Himself out of the control and dominion of darkness and has transferred me into the kingdom of the Son of His love (Colossians 1:12–13).

✝ Since I have been raised with Christ to a new life, I aim at and seek the rich eternal treasures that are above, where Christ is seated at the right hand of God. I set my mind and keep it set on what is above, not on the things that are on the earth. For as far as this world is concerned, I have died and my new real life is hidden with Christ in God (1 Corinthians 1:30).

✝ Therefore, I have considered the members of my body dead to immorality, impurity, passion, evil desire and greed. I put away and rid myself of anger, rage, bad feelings toward others, curses and slander and abusive speech from my mouth (Colossians 3:5, 8).

✝ I let my speech at all times be gracious, pleasant and winsome, seasoned with salt, so that I may never be at a loss to know how I ought to answer anyone who puts a question to me. I clothe myself, as God's chosen one, purified, holy and well loved by God Himself by putting on behavior marked by tender hearted pity and mercy, kind feelings, a lowly opinion of myself, gentle ways and patience which is tireless and long suffering, and has the power to endure whatever comes, with good temper (Colossians 3:12).

✝ I look carefully how I walk. I live purposefully and worthily and accurately, not as the unwise and witless, but as a wise sensible, intelligent person, making the very most of the time, buying up each opportunity because the days are evil. Therefore, I am not vague, thoughtless, and foolish but I understand and firmly grasp what the will of the Lord is (Ephesians 5:15–16).

✝ I will establish myself in righteousness and I will be far from even the thought of oppression or destruction for I shall not fear, and far from terror for it shall not come near me (Isaiah 54:14).

✝ I listen to God's Word, therefore, I live securely and I'm at ease from the dread of evil (Proverbs 1:33).

✝ I thank You, Lord, that my love abounds still more and more in knowledge and all discernment, that

I approve the things that are excellent and that I am sincere and without offense until the day of Christ (Philippians 1:9).

✝ I am a child of God by faith in Christ Jesus (Galatians 3:26).

✝ Father, I present my body to You as a living and holy sacrifice acceptable to You, which is my spiritual service of worship. I will not be conformed to this world, but transformed by the renewing of my mind, that I may prove what the will of God is (Romans 12:1–2).

✝ I have the mind of Christ; therefore I can know the thoughts of my Lord that He may instruct me (I Corinthians 2:16).

✝ I am renewed in the spirit of my mind and I put on the new self, which in the likeness of God, has been created in righteousness and holiness of the truth (Ephesians 4:23–24).

✝ Father, I thank You that I do not have a spirit of fear, but I have a spirit of power, a spirit of love and a spirit of a sound, strong, firm, safe, stable and disciplined mind which produces Godly thoughts (2 Timothy 1:7).

✝ I set my mind to believe, bear, hope and endure all things (I Corinthians 13:7).

- ✝ I set my mind on things above, not on things on the earth (Colossians 3:2).

- ✝ I am strong and courageous, I will not fear or tremble or be dismayed. God's Word will never stop being spoken out of my mouth, for I meditate on the Word of God day and night and I am careful to do all that God commands, therefore success and prosperity are mine now (Joshua 1:5–9).

- ✝ I am established in righteousness. I am far from oppression in my mind; and fear and terror will not come near me to control me. No weapon formed against me shall prosper and every tongue that accuses me in judgment shall be shown to be in the wrong (Isaiah 54:14, 17).

- ✝ I let the peace of God rule in my heart and mind and I am thankful to God in all things (Colossians 3:15).

- ✝ Father, I thank You that the peace of God, which surpasses all knowledge, is guarding my heart and mind in Christ Jesus. I command my mind to dwell only on that which is true, honorable, pure, lovely excellent and worthy of praise (Philippians 4:7-8).

- ✝ I have the mind of Christ (1 Corinthians 2:16).

- ✝ I am the head and not the tail, I am above and not below (Deuteronomy 28:13).

- ✝ For God has not given us a spirit of fear, but of power and of love and of a sound mind (2 Timothy 1:7).

- ✝ I let all men know and perceive and recognize my unselfishness, my considerateness, and my forbearing spirit (Philippians 4:5).

- ✝ I declare today that death and life are in the power of my tongue and I use my tongue to produce the life of God in my body (Proverbs 18:21).

- ✝ My body is the temple of the Holy Spirit and I glorify God in it by walking in divine healing and divine health (1 Corinthians 6:19).

- ✝ I am redeemed from the curse, no curse of sickness and disease can dwell in my body or in my life; Christ redeemed me from the curse of the law, having become a curse for me. "For cursed is one who hangs on a tree; therefore, the blessing of Abraham comes to me now in Jesus' name" (Galatians 3:13–14)!

HERE ARE SOME TRUTHS:

- ✝ I declare full recovery over my body: "Behold, I give you the authority to trample on serpents and scorpions, and over all the power of the enemy, and nothing shall by any means hurt you" (Luke 10:19).

✝ For You O Lord, will bless the righteous; with favor You will surround him as with a shield (Psalm 5:12).

✝ For the Lord is righteous, He loves righteousness;

✝ His countenance beholds the upright (Psalm 11:7). The eyes of the Lord are on the righteous, and His ears are open to their cry (Psalm 34:15).

✝ The righteous cry out, and the Lord hears, and delivers them out of all their troubles (Psalm 34:17, 19).

✝ Evil shall slay the wicked, and those who hate the righteous shall be condemned (Psalm 34:21).

✝ For the arms of the wicked shall be broken, but the Lord upholds the righteous (Psalm 37:17).

✝ The righteous shall inherit the land, and dwell in it forever (Psalm 37:29).

✝ The mouth of the righteous speaks wisdom (Psalm 37:30).

✝ Cast your burden on the Lord, and He shall sustain you; He shall never permit the righteous to be moved (Psalm 55:22).

The following Affirmations are from The Sure Foundation Theological Institute.[18]

Now take hold of the following topics by putting your name where it says, "YOUR NAME."

EMPOWERMENT

Behold, I give you the power to tread on serpents and scorpions, and over all the power of the enemy: and nothing shall hurt you by any means. (Luke 10:19)

But ye shall receive power, after that the Holy Ghost has come upon you: and you shall be witnesses unto me both in Jerusalem, and in all Judaea, Samaria, and the uttermost part of the earth. (Acts 1:8)

I, YOUR NAME, do ardently declare and affirm my acknowledgment of God's promise of empowerment to me. I further demonstrate my openness to receive God's power for my life. "Much more they which receive abundance of grace and the gift of righteousness shall reign in life by one, Jesus Christ" (Romans 5:17)

For it is God who works in you both to will and do his good pleasure. (Philippians 2:13)

That he would grant you, according to the riches of his glory, to be strengthened with might by his Spirit in the inner man; (Ephesians 3:16)

I, YOUR NAME, further affirm my worthiness through the blood of Christ to receive God's empowerment in my life. Father in Heaven, I now pray that you would strengthen me by the power of your might in my inner man, that I might be able to do your will with enthusiasm. "in all these things, we are more than conquerors through him that loved us" Romans 8:37

And, behold, I send the promise of my Father upon you: but tarry you in the city of Jerusalem, until you be endued with power from on high. (Luke 24:49)

And when he (Sampson) came unto Lehi, the Philistines shouted against him: and the Spirit of the Lord came mightily upon him, And he found a new jawbone of an ass, and put forth his hand, and took it, and slew a thousand men in addition to that. (Judges 15:14-15)

I further ask you to empower me to accomplish the dreams and goals that you have given me for my life.

MY CALLING

And we know that all things work together for good to those who love God and those who are called according to his purpose. For whom he did foreknow, he also did predestinate to be conformed to the image of his Son, that he might be the firstborn among many brethren. Moreover, whom he did predestinate, them he also called: and whom he called, them he also justified: and whom he justified, them he also glorified. (Romans 8:28-30)

I, YOUR NAME, am one who loves God and is called according to His purposes. May the calling of Christ in my life become more and more clear to me that I might fulfill my destiny in Him.

I affirm myself to be crucified with Christ and resurrected with Christ into the newness of life through my profession of faith in Him. I also profess and confirm that I will fulfill and know my calling daily.

I, YOUR NAME, agree with the scripture in Romans 8:28 that All Things Work Together for my Good. Therefore, I decree that all things are working together for my good and that I will know and fulfill my calling, Amen.

But the God of all grace, who hath called us unto his eternal glory by Christ Jesus, after you have suffered a while, make you perfect, establish, strengthen, settle you. (1 Peter 5:10)

Who hath saved us, and called us with a holy calling, not according to our works, but according to his purpose and grace, which was given us in Christ Jesus before the world began, (2 Tim 1:9).

MOTIVATION

Not slothful in business; fervent in spirit; serving the Lord; (Romans 12:11)

I, YOUR NAME, am resurrected in Christ to be motivated to get busy with the assignment handed to me from on high. I am dead to slackness and putting things off that should be done now. I must work the works of Him that sent me while it is day: the night comes when no man can work. (John 9:4) And he said unto them, How is it that you sought me? Did you not know that I must be about my Father's business? (Luke 2:49)

I, YOUR NAME, am delivered in Christ from the hindrance of the enemy. I believe God has opened a door for me that no man can close, and I SHALL EXCEL with God's opportunity. By God's grace, in Jesus's name, Amen. I thank you, Lord, for your promise of reward. And, behold, I come quickly; my reward is with me, to give every man according to his work. (Revelation 22:12)

Why are you in despair, my soul? And why are you restless within me? Wait for God, for I will again praise Him for the help of His presence, my God. (Psalm 42:5)

With goodwill doing service, as to the Lord, and not to men: Knowing that whatever good thing any man does, the same shall receive of the Lord, whether bond or free. (Ephesians 6:7-8)

How long will you lie down, you lazy one? When will you arise from your sleep? A little sleep, a little slumber, a little folding of the hands to rest, then your poverty will come in like a draught, and your need like an armed man. (Proverbs 6:9-11 & 24:33-34)

BLESSING MAGNET

And all these blessings will come to you and reach you if you obey the voice of the Lord thy God. (Deuteronomy 28:2-14)

I, YOUR NAME, am a blessing magnet. Blessings overtake me. (Deuteronomy 28:2) I decree and affirm my right and privilege to inherit and receive God's blessings on my life.

Blessed be the God and Father of our Lord Jesus Christ, who hath blessed us with all spiritual blessings in heavenly places in Christ (Ephesians 1:3)

But thanks be to God, who gives us the victory through our Lord Jesus Christ. (1 Corinthians 15:57)

You are from God, little children, and have overcome them: because greater is He who is in you than he that is in the world. (I John 4:4)

I, YOUR NAME, through this affirmation, profess my faith in the fact that I am a beneficiary and an inheritor. I am victorious, I am a winner, I am an overcomer, I am the head, not the tail, above ONLY and not beneath (Deuteronomy 28:13). I further affirm that I am healthy and wealthy in

Christ and that I have favor with God and man. (Deuteronomy 8:18) It is so, so be it in Jesus' name.

"Blessings are upon the head of the just" (Proverbs 10:6)

Even by the God of your father, who shall help you; and by the Almighty, who shall bless you with blessings of heaven above, blessings of the deep that lie under, blessings of the breasts, and the womb (Genesis 49:25)

A faithful man shall abound with blessings, but he who does not haste to be rich shall not be innocent. (Proverbs 28:20)

"I shall come in the fullness of the blessing of the gospel of Christ" (Romans 15:29)

The cup of blessing which we bless, is it not the communion of the blood of Christ? The bread which we break, is it not the communion of the body of Christ? (1 Corinthians 10:16)

For ye know the grace of our Lord Jesus Christ, that, though he was rich, yet for our sakes, he became poor, that ye through his poverty might be rich. (Corinthians 8:9)

THE DEVIL IS DEFEATED

"You have overcome the wicked one "(I John 2:13-14)

'Forasmuch then as the children are partakers of flesh and blood, he likewise took part of the same; that through death he might destroy him that had the power of death, that is, the devil." (Hebrews 2:14)

The Lord Jesus Christ defeated the devil and destroyed his works. Therefore, I, YOUR NAME, repent from trying to do what Jesus already did. I will not attempt to add to the work of the Cross of Christ with my dead work of trying to conquer the devil. I acknowledge that the devil is defeated in Christ.

"For this purpose, the Son of God was manifested, that he might destroy the works of the devil" (I John 3:8)

I, YOUR NAME, affirm and decree that I am dead in Christ to the devil and resurrected unto God. I a.m. delivered from the power of darkness and translated into the kingdom of God's dear Son. I HAVE overcome the devil through the Blood of the Lamb and the word of my testimony. It is finished in Christ. I decide to abide and rest from my labors in the work of Christ. Thank you, Lord, for the victory. I do not have to get it; I have it in Jesus' name.

"Who has delivered us from the power of darkness, and has translated us into the kingdom of his dear Son:" (Colossians 1:13)

"And having spoiled principalities and powers, he made a shew of them openly, triumphing over them in it." (Colossians 2:15)

"Behold, I give unto you power to tread on serpents and scorpions, and over all the power of the enemy: and nothing shall by any means hurt you." (Luke 10:19)

I am seated in Heavenly Places — FAR— above all power and principality and dominion and every name that is named. I cast down every imagination and high thing that exalts itself against the knowledge of God, of who I am and where I am in Christ Jesus!

"Which he wrought in Christ, when he raised him from the dead, and set him at his right hand in the heavenly places, Far above all principality, and power, and might, and dominion, and every name that is named, not only in this world but also in that which is to come." (Ephesians 1:20-21) "And hath raised us up together, and made us sit together in heavenly places in Christ Jesus" (Ephesians 2:6) "Casting down imaginations, and every high thing that exalts itself against the knowledge of God, and bringing into captivity every thought to the obedience of Christ" (2 Corinthians 10:5)

RAISE THE BAR

I press toward the mark for the prize of the high calling of
God in Christ Jesus. (Philippians 3:14)

This is a faithful saying, and these things I will that you constantly affirm, that they which have believed in God might be careful to maintain good works. These things are good and profitable unto men. (Titus 3:8)

I, YOUR NAME, with the presence of the Holy Spirit and the Lord Jesus Christ, declare and affirm before the Father in Heaven that I, with God's help, decide to raise the bar. I will now hold a higher standard of excellence so that I may excel in God's plan for my life.

Enlarge the place of your tent, and let them stretch forth the curtains of your habitations: spare not, lengthen my cords, and strengthen my stakes; For you will break forth on the right hand and the left. (Isaiah 54:2-3)

Not slothful in business; fervent in spirit; serving the Lord, (Romans 12:11)

I, YOUR NAME, further declare and acknowledge that I am capable and willing to make changes necessary to raise the standard and expedite my quest's vision. With a pen in hand, I will write or underscore new standards for my life, i.e., daily prayer, confession, exercise, eating right, being on time, completing my goals, etc. Finally, I decided to stay out of the land of mediocrity. Amen!

SALVATION FOR OTHERS

"Therefore, I also, after I heard of your faith in the Lord Jesus and your love for all the saints, do not cease to give thanks for you, making mention of you in my prayers: that the

God of our Lord Jesus Christ, the Father of glory, may give to you (them) the spirit of wisdom and revelation in the knowledge of Him, the eyes of your (their) understanding being enlightened; that you may know what the hope of His calling is, what are the riches of the glory of His inheritance in the saints, and what is the exceeding greatness of His power toward us who believe, according to the working of His mighty power which He worked in Christ when He raised Him from the dead and seated Him at His right hand in the heavenly places, far above all principality and power and might and dominion, and every name that is named, not only in this age but also in that which is to come. And He put all things under His feet and gave Him to be head over all things to the church, His body, the fullness of Him who fills all in all (Ephesians 1:15–23).

I pray as an intercessor for (SAY THEIR NAME) the ones whom I love. May the eyes of their understanding be enlightened to the TRUTH, according to the matchless power of the Holy Spirit. I call (SAY THEIR NAME) dead to darkness and resurrected to the light.

Thank you for reading,
An Injection of Faith: One Addict's Journey to Deliverance.

Gaining exposure as an independent author relies primarily on word-of-mouth, so if you have the time and inclination, please consider leaving a short-written review wherever you can.

It also helps others when considering the book.

Thank you

Review Links:

link.anthonyordille.com/ReviewChannel

If you found this book helpful, please let anyone you know struggling with an addiction know where they can get a copy.

Available Drug and Alcohol Program Hotlines:

The following groups can be contacted for help should you need assistance with drug and/or alcohol problems. But remember, it does not stop here.

National Council on Alcoholism Information Line
800-NCA-CALL – www.ncadd.org

The National Council on Alcoholism Inc. (NCA) is a national nonprofit organization combating alcoholism, other drug addictions, and related problems. It provides information about NCA's state and local affiliates, activities in their areas, and referral services to families and individuals seeking help with alcohol or other problems.

Substance Abuse and Mental Health Services Administration
800-662-HELP – www.samhsa.gov

The SAMHSA Helpline is a confidential, free, twenty-four-hour-a-day, 365-day-a-year information service provided in English and Spanish for individuals and family members facing substance abuse issues. This service provides referrals to local treatment facilities, support groups, and community-based organizations. Callers can also order free publications and other information in print on substance abuse and mental health issues.

Visit www.findtreatment.gov for a treatment center near you or a loved one needing help.

Suicide Information[19]

Information is taken from the National Institute of Mental Health website19

Suicide is a major, preventable public health problem. In 2019 Suicide was the tenth leading cause of death in the United States, claiming the lives of over 47,500 people.

The overall rate was 13.9 suicide deaths per 100,000 people. An estimated 11 attempted suicides occur per every suicide death.

Suicidal behavior is complex. Some risk factors vary with age, gender, or ethnic group and may occur in combination or change over time.

What are the risk factors for suicide?

Research shows that risk factors for suicide include:

- depression and other mental disorders, or a substance abuse disorder (often in combination with other mental disorders). More than 90 percent of people who commit suicide have these risk factors
- prior suicide attempt
- family history of mental disorder or substance abuse
- family history of suicide
- family violence, including physical or sexual abuse
- firearms in the home, in 2019, firearms were the most common method used in suicide deaths in the United States,

accounting for a little over half of all suicide deaths (23,941)
- incarceration
- exposure to the suicidal behavior of others, such as family members, peers, or media figures

However, suicide and suicidal behavior are not normal responses to stress; many people have these risk factors but are not suicidal. Research also shows that the risk for suicide is associated with changes in brain chemicals called neurotransmitters, including serotonin. Decreased serotonin levels have been found in people with depression, impulsive disorders, a history of suicide attempts, and the brains of suicide victims.

If you are in a crisis and need help right away:

Call this toll-free number, available 24 hours a day, every day: 1-800-273-TALK (8255).

You will reach the National Suicide Prevention Lifeline, a service available to anyone. You may call for yourself or for someone you care about. All calls are confidential.

Resources

Please feel free to send me your testimonies on how you enjoyed the book and what the Lord is doing in your life. And please let me know how God delivered you from your addictions through the power of salvation. You will find our contact information on my website.

If you know of anyone who would benefit from reading this book, please share the title with them so they can get a copy. Thanks.

Between the first edition in 2013 and this revised edition, I wrote another book and a workbook and developed a Christ-Centered 12-step program called Addiction-Free Life (AFL for short).

The guidebook was written with the hope that it will help those who are struggling with addictions and show that there is a better way to recover, as I mentioned in this book. It is not just for alcoholics or drug addicts; it is designed to help those struggling with addictions of all kinds. Most addicts are directed to a traditional twelve-step program, but for those who want to lean on the truth about God, there is another way to an Addiction-Free Life.

AFL will show you that way! As long as you keep the faith and follow the direction given, you stand a great chance of beating the addiction that holds you captive. The workbook was created to come alongside the guidebook and help you work through the 12 steps.

Addiction-Free Life is based in the
United States of America

Other Books by this Author

Please visit your favorite book retailer to discover other books by Anthony Ordille @ link.anthonyordille.com/Authorcentral or wherever books are sold.

Autobiography
An Injection of Faith: One Addict's Journey to Deliverance

Addiction
Overcome Addiction by God's Grace: 12-Steps to Freedom
Overcome Addiction by God's Grace: 12-Steps to Freedom Workbook
Breaking the Chains of Addiction: An Introduction to Addiction-Free Life
The 5 Essential Ways to Living Addiction-Free—Free Report

Christian Living
My Daily Scriptures: A Day by Day Bible Reading Guide—Here is a book that will help you read the Bible in a year, cover-to-cover, book-by-book.
My Daily Scriptures 365 Day Journal—Companion to guide book or as a standalone journal.

Biblical Fiction Novels
Messiah's Preparation: A Christian Historical Fiction of Jesus in the Wilderness—Previously published as *The Itinerary*.

You may also find the links to these books @ www.anthonyordille.com/

Connect with Anthony Ordille

Addiction-Free Life is based in the United States of America

Send all inquiries through the website at:
www.anthonyordille.com

I appreciate you reading my book! You can connect with me through my website, www.anthonyordille.com, or link.anthonyordille.com/ConnectLandingPage.

Photos

The Author Growing Up

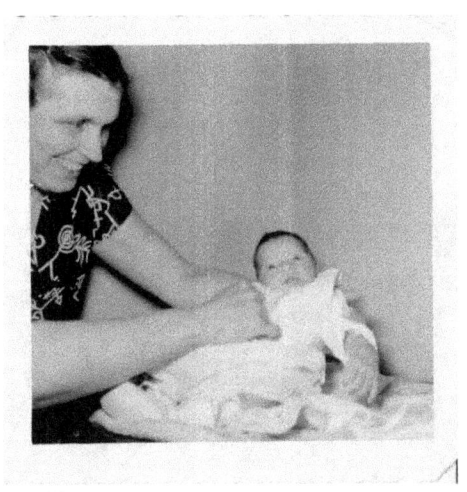

One month old

Six months old

Age three, my sisters dressed me up for a Halloween parade. See why I had issues!

Age six

Age eleven

Age thirteen, losing the tie

Age fourteen, losing tie and jacket

Age twenty-three, losing mind

Age fifty-three, suit and tie return

Age fifty-six

Age twelve with my mom and dad

Age three, waiting for my dad to wake up

First best Christmas with my daughter, nine,
and son, eleven

My adopted son, age seven.
He loved his boots and hat

That is me holding onto my mom

My dad, mom and Matt, dad #2

Having some fun, who needs drugs when you have the joy of the Lord!

Serenity medallion after rehab

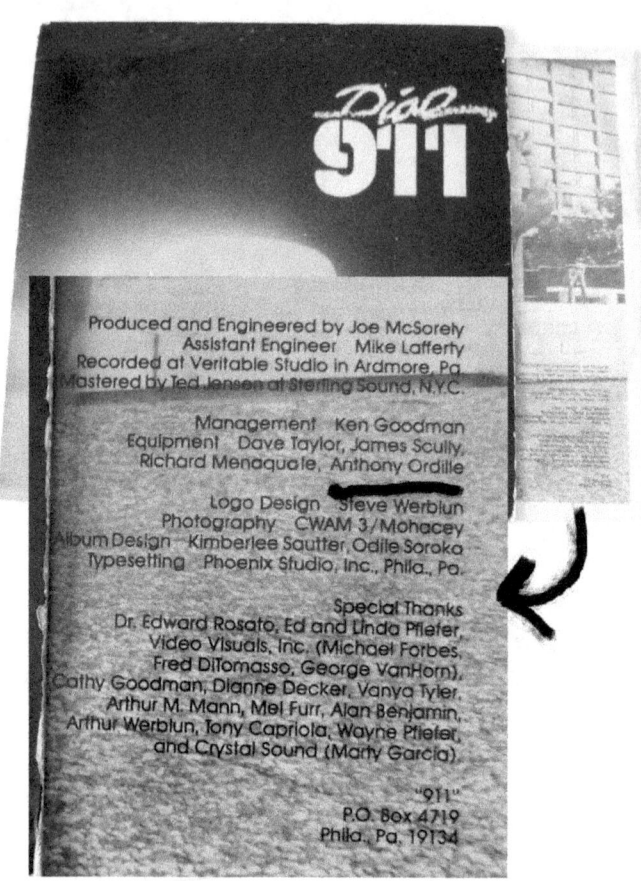

911 band, My name is underlined

Up-to-date train set

Videotaping a basketball game in high school

[1] Used by permission. His Hands Ministries Fellowship Inc. All Rights Reserved. PO BOX 337, New Gretna, NJ 08224. www.his-handsfellowship.com/.

[2] Used by permission. 110 Grapevine Highway, Suite 101 | Hurst, TX 76054 | United States of America. www.kingdomglobal.com.

[3] Alcoholics Anonymous is an international fellowship of men and women who have had a drinking problem. www.aa.org.

[4] Narcotics Anonymous is a global, community-based organization with a multi-lingual and multicultural membership. www.na.org.

[5] Based on The Random House Dictionary, Classic Edition, Copyright © 1983 by Random House Inc. All rights reserved.

[6] Based on The Random House Dictionary, Classic Edition, Copyright © 1983 by Random House Inc. All rights reserved. pp. 274-275, 1003, 387-388.

[7] Based on The Random House Dictionary, Classic Edition, Copyright © 1983 by Random House Inc. All rights reserved. pp. 10.

[8] Merriam-Webster Online Dictionary, Copyright © 2015 by Merriam-Webster, Incorporated. All rights reserved.

[9] Dial 911 Released 1981 by Devotion Music, ltd. World Wide Records. All rights reserved. Produced by Joe McSorely. Recorded at Veritable Studio in Ardmore, PA.
Artist: John Masi, Dan Michael, Michael Rosato, Special appearance David Columbo.

[10] www.drugabuse.gov Accessed on multiple occasions. National Institute on Drug Abuse, 3WFN MSC 6024, 301 North Stonestreet Ave Bethesda, MD 20892, 301-443-1124 (general inquiries), 301-443-6245 (press inquiries).

[11] Copyright © 1982, 1983, 1984, 1986, 1987, 1988 by Narcotics Anonymous World Services, Inc. All rights reserved. Quote taken from the Fifth Edition, page 26.

[12] Merriam-Webster Online Dictionary Copyright © 2015 by Merriam-Webster, Incorporated. All rights reserved.

[13] "The Origin of our Serenity Prayer" by www.aahistory.com/prayer.html Retrieved July 14, 2008.

[14] Copyright © 1982, 1983, 1984, 1986, 1987, 1988 by Narcotics Anonymous World Services, Inc. All rights reserved. Quote taken from the Fifth Edition, page 17.

[15] Webster's Dictionary of the English Language, Based on The Random House Dictionary, Classic Edition, Copyright © 1983 by Random House Inc. All rights reserved. pp. 101.

[16] Webster's Dictionary of the English Language, Based on The Random House Dictionary, Classic Edition, Copyright © 1983 by Random House Inc. All rights reserved. pp. 802.

[17] Websters's New World Dictionary, Third College Edition, © 1988 by Simon & Schuster, Inc. pp. 22.

[18] The Sure Foundation Theological Institute 2010 © www.theologicalinstitute.com Used by permission by Rev. Marc Stolman.

[19] https://www.nimh.nih.gov/health/statistics/suicide, accessed 5/11/2022.

www.ingramcontent.com/pod-product-compliance
Lightning Source LLC
Chambersburg PA
CBHW070617300426
44113CB00010B/1569